Using Friction to Grow is a reminder that faith isn't about ease—it's about endurance, love, and growth. These women stayed, wrestled, and found strength in the struggle. Their courage inspires all of us to hold on to what's good while working to make it better.

— Steve Young
Hall of fame NFL quarterback,
humanitarian and author of *The Law of Love*

I loved how *Using Friction to Grow* celebrates women who stayed rooted in faith while stretching toward possibility. I'll be sharing it with my daughters, friends, and every woman learning to trust her own divine direction.

—Kristin Andrus
CEO of Gathering for Impact,
Chairman Andrus Foundation

Using Friction to Grow documents courageous role models whose voices and stories will inspire generations of women to nurture their talents. I am excited to share this book with friends, particularly friends who are discerning their vocations to contribute to the public sphere yet lack proximate role models.

—Miranda Wilcox
Associate Professor of English at Brigham Young University,
Co-editor of *Standing Apart: Mormon Historical
Consciousness and the Concept of Apostasy*

This book is filled with the inspiring stories of Latter-day Saint women who took unique, courageous, and transformative paths—in the face of friction—that were rooted in personal revelation and conviction to their faith. This is a must-read for anyone seeking faith-based examples of how to live a life of conviction, boldness, perseverance, grace, hope, and purpose!

—Susan Madsen
Professor of Organizational Leadership,
Director, Utah Women & Leadership Project,
Jon M. Huntsman School of Business, Utah State University

Where was this book when I was in my 20s and 30s? I will be recommending it to every woman of faith who dreams of an 'and' life—who's all-in on the Gospel, all-in on family, and all-in on her work. Inspiring!

—Whitney Johnson
CEO of Disruption Advisors,
Thinkers50 Leading Management Thinker,
Host of the *Disrupt Yourself* podcast

Many are so challenged by the angst of our age. We sometimes fall into a belief that we are the only generation that had it so. Robin Ritch's beautiful book is a reminder that the generation or two before us struggled with challenges similar in size and significance to our own time. Structural, cultural, and traditional barriers were the rule of the day. I can't wait for my children but also my college students to read this.

—Dr. Lynne Hilton Wilson
Associate Professor of Ancient
Scripture at Brigham Young University,
Author of *Christ's Emancipation of New Testament Women,
Nativity Narratives*, and *Learning the Language of the Lord:
A Guidebook to Personal Revelation,*
Co-founder of Scripture Central

The 70s were a time characterized by many of the issues we face (sadly) in our own time. If anything, the issues were less subtle and more pervasive: race, women's roles, marriage, role of the church, leadership in the church and more. Robin's beautiful book draws out the lessons we can use today as we listen to the wonderful voices of women who faced such times with grace, forgiveness, patience...and resolution for change. They resisted the structural, cultural, and traditional barriers of their day...and overcame them with resilient faith and love. I'm excited to share their lessons with our wonderful children as they each develop their own path forward.

—Dow R Wilson
Former CEO and current Chairman
of the Board of Varian Systems,
Former Area Seventy for the Church of
Jesus Christ of Latter-day Saints

Ritch weaves together powerful narratives of tension, faith, and growth. They are anchored in faith and conviction. I've long felt a gap in biographies of modern, faithful Latter-day Saint women, and I'm grateful for Robin Ritch's thoughtful work in helping to bridge it.

—Mary Stallings
Author and founder of *Come Follow Me Daily*

Using Friction to Grow was extremely insightful and eye opening. Though separated by decades, I felt so much empathy for these women. The struggles and friction we feel as women in society (and in many religions) transcends time. How do we reconcile what we feel called to do from the innermost parts of our soul to what the bounds of culture tells us we can do? The stories shared within the pages of this book eloquently illustrate how taxing this dilemma can be while showing that determined women come out on the other side—stronger, more resilient, more faithful. As a mother of three daughters and a CEO, I recognize we've come a long way, but I know there is still a long way to go. This book is a fantastic conversation starter. I'm excited to share *Using Friction to Grow* with my husband and other men as we collectively break down barriers of culture to make the world a place that accepts the dreams, talents, passions, and skill sets of women in the same way they do men.

—Mackenzie Bauer
Co-founder of Thread Wallets,
Forbes 30 under 30, and community champion

Using Friction to Grow

BCC PRESS

By Common Consent Press is a non-profit publisher dedicated to producing affordable, high-quality books that help define and shape the Latter-day Saint experience. BCC Press publishes books that address all aspects of Mormon life. Our mission includes finding manuscripts that will contribute to the lives of thoughtful Latter-day Saints, mentoring authors and nurturing projects to completion, and distributing important books to the Mormon audience at the lowest possible cost.

Using Friction to Grow

STORIES OF STRENGTH & RESILIENCE
LDS WOMEN 1968–1976

ROBIN RITCH

For information contact
By Common Consent Press
972 East Burnham Lane
Draper, Utah 84020

Cover design: D Christian Harrison
Book design: Andrew Heiss

www.bccpress.org

ISBN-13: 978-1-961471-32-0

10 9 8 7 6 5 4 3 2 1

To the women who went before—who bore the weight of silence, questioned, believed, and endured. Your courage taught me that friction is not a stopping point, but a holy invitation to grow

Contents

Contents

Preface

||||||||||||||||||||||||||||||||

Why does nature reveal truth and patterns? I recently kayaked from the redwood forest to the ocean. While there, I recognized that redwoods, also known as "the giants," are a complex and beautiful phenomenon. Their endurance and majesty are breathtaking. One of the most interesting things about redwoods is that they are so big and so old that younger trees and plants live on their branches and trunks. As you walk through redwood forests, you see many types of trees and even new redwoods growing out of older ones. New trees literally grow on the shoulders of these giants.

On the shoulders of giants. This phrase rings in my head as I consider some questions. Who are my giants? On whom can I build my tree? Who is relatable to me? Who are the women who relied upon their own relationship with Christ and their own personal revelation to stay in an organization that caused friction in their lives? How did they find their unique path and stay on it in the face of such ambiguity and challenge?

Recently, I spoke with Christine Durham, retired Chief Justice of the Supreme Court of Utah, about her journey and how she followed her path despite prevailing cultural norms. She shared a lot of personal experiences, but what particularly stood out was that her group of friends had a real connection to the early twentieth-century LDS women who led in the community, at home, and in the Church. Her generation was able to see a path forward because of these women who were her grandmother's age—and yet still relatable. As Justice Durham said this, it struck me that young LDS women today (twenty to forty years old) do not have a link to a generation of women that were allowed to lead in the church and were focused on following their unique paths, regardless of cultural norms. These women exist, but the younger generation does not know their stories. Bringing to light a group of women who focused on using their unique strengths in their communities, homes, and other forums, who used their inner voices to move forward, is a story that must be told before it is lost.

To find these stories, I interviewed LDS women who were innovators in their chosen fields, who lived through the Equal Rights Amendment ("ERA") era in the United States, and who have chosen to stay as participating members in their faith. I focused on women who were making their "and" decisions during the tumultuous period of 1968–1974. By "and," I mean they were deciding to be married, to have kids, *and* to do something else outside the home. I wanted to understand how these women followed their own journey regardless of their Church leaders' view of what constituted an "ideal" life for women. I hoped there might be something about how these women followed their paths that could relate to women today. I interviewed women who purposefully chose to be mothers *and* to also use their unique strengths to innovate in forums outside the home.

I'm not the only one asking these types of questions. Recently I have found myself in countless conversations with LDS women in their 20s or 30s who are grappling with what they perceive as a choice between their own unique path and the expectations of their faith community. They're wondering, "How do I stay in a faith community that sets up an ideal path for women that is not my path?" Because they lack role models, many of these women conclude that the result of this dichotomy is a choice between faith and their own unique path. It's one or the other, and many are choosing to leave the faith. They don't realize that "and" is an option. They don't know that women have faced these choices before, in a different time and context, and were able to choose "and" and have all the wonder that comes with following the path they feel called to take and continuing to bask in the benefits that come from being a member of our LDS faith community.

Women in their 20s remind me of the generation of women I interviewed and how they talked about the late 1960s and early 1970s. Like today, there was tremendous social upheaval and consequently not a clear path forward. Like today, these women had options for education and employment that were not available to prior generations. Linking the two generations together by sharing their stories, hopefully will allow the rising generation to stand on the shoulders of giants, as this rising generation figures out how to use their agency and reconcile the social issues of the times with the complexity of choices and their faith community. We need to share how they knew to use their agency to reconcile the social issues of the times with the complexity of choices and their faith community. We need to bring these two generations together.

So, I'm bringing them together. Here are models of women that dealt with the complexity of choice and were able to move forward in a way that gave them the very best in life. These women remain firmly anchored in the gospel of Jesus Christ and have pursued paths that compelled them to spread their light and influence outside the home. Let's learn from women that have forged this path before, who used their agency to pursue what was best for them.

I started with the thesis that we need the narratives of the current "grandmother" generation to understand how we can continue to follow our unique path when social justice (and other) issues conflict with the LDS community. As I interviewed these women, I found more than I bargained for. Since I was in diapers during the time which they were making their decisions, I didn't realize until I began my research how many nuances there were to understand. Each woman valued unique parts of their faith community, and all experienced friction, whether or not it was inside or outside the Church. I was left with a rich understanding of how these women experienced friction coming from multiple sources, including their religious community, and yet found a way to coexist with their fellow Saints despite that friction.

The women I interviewed lived in different locations and had different experiences; each had unique key takeaways from their experience with friction. As I talked with them, I grew to understand why it's important to build on the shoulders of giants. When you walk among these giants, you feel dwarfed by their towering height, grandeur, and ageless beauty—but also inspired. I hope you will find in their stories the awe-inspiring peace that comes from standing in a grove of redwoods.

Understanding Life
for LDS Women
from 1968 to 1976

As I interviewed these women, it became clear that I needed to fully understand the era in which they made their pivotal decisions regarding family, education, and outside-the-home interests. To extract insights from how these pioneering women dealt with friction, we must first understand the 1970s milieu in the United States.

Members of the Church in the '60s and '70s, specifically women, confronted a cultural maelstrom. Young Americans in their teens and twenties were revolting against current policies, structures, and the out-of-touch previous generation—not unlike what we've seen in the 2020s. The sexual revolution was in full swing; anti-war protests and civil rights were perpetual hot buttons. The result was a lot of chaos, but a good deal of perceived progress as well. The women's movement took off, and many declared the 1970s to be The Decade of The Woman. So-called "progressive" women fought against the inequality between the sexes and demanded the right to have their own checking account, credit card, and equal pay, as well as access to education, financial aid and scholarships, birth control and abortion. An entire generation of youth were engaged in what they believed was a crusade to create a better society. It was the first time in the United States when one generation led the charge to change the playing field for those on the margins. The air was electrified with activism and a sense of transformation. In one woman's words, it was a time when "we thought we could make real change, and it felt exciting."[1]

There was also a seismic shift in demographics: where people lived, accessed education, how and where people worked, and even the makeup of families. Prior to 1960, "stay-at-home mom" wasn't an expression that was commonly used. A personification of the perfect wife and mother, June Cleaver in TV's *Leave It to Beaver* greeted her husband every night in high heels, a string of pearls, a dress, and a made-from-scratch dinner. Much of the turmoil of the 1960s and '70s was a backlash against the idealized household of the '50s.

As I was too young to be mindful of the dynamics of these two decades, I was unaware of the resistance and friction LDS women of that generation faced within their own faith community—not just on women's rights, but also racial inequality.

---

1. (Durham, 2023)

The LDS Church, Race, and the Civil Rights Movement

The Civil Rights movement took up the whole breadth of the 1960s and into the '70s. Marked by a sea change of new laws giving Black Americans expanded civil rights, this movement encountered opposition from many quarters, including The Church of Jesus Christ of Latter-day Saints.

A series of landmark laws were enacted by the US Congress, largely in response to years of struggle and protests, that tried to tackle different areas of discrimination. In 1964, the U.S. Congress passed the Civil Rights Act, which outlawed discrimination on the basis of race, color, religion, sex, or national origin. A year later, Congress enacted the Voting Rights Act, which prohibited discrimination in voting practices and procedures. In 1968, Congress passed the Fair Housing Act, which outlawed discrimination in the rental, sale, or financing of housing based on race, color, religion, or national origin. These laws were instrumental in providing legal protection to Black Americans and other marginalized groups. Despite the passage of these laws, however, their application was not uniform across the country. Many states and local governments continued to enforce discriminatory practices, and it took several years of legal battles and social activism to fully enforce these laws.

In addition to being a time of monumental legal changes, 1964–1978 also saw significant social and cultural revolutions, as Black Americans and other marginalized groups fought for greater equality and recognition. The Civil Rights Movement, led by figures such as Martin Luther King Jr., Rosa Parks, Ella

1900–1930	1930s	1940s	1950s	1960s	1970s
Women: no bank accounts, no credit cards, no loans, access to equal education, rape/domestic violence laws non-existent, discrimation on pay/hiring/jobs, could get fired for being pregnant, couldn't serve on juries in all 50 states					
Women working: Farms, industrial, community	Anybody that could work worked	Anybody that could work worked	Rise of "stay at home moms" in certain demographics	"Stay at home moms" in certain demographics	Women starting to work in all demographics
Community and extended families	Community and extended families	Community and extended families	Nuclear families		
Suffragette movement	Great Depression	World War II	Suburbanization and media		
The "Great Migration"			Civil Rights Movement		
				Anti-War Movement	
				Women's Rights Movement	

Baker, Fannie Lou Hamer, Diane Nash, and Shirley Chisholm, helped raise awareness of the injustices faced by Black Americans and mobilized public support for change.

Until 1978, the LDS Church had maintained a policy that excluded Black men of African descent from holding the priesthood and barred Black people from participating in temple ordinances. This policy also impacted Brigham Young University (BYU), as it is owned and operated by the LDS Church.

In the late 1960s and early '70s, some athletic opponents of BYU protested against the Church's racial policies. A notable protest was the "Black 14" incident in 1969, when fourteen Black members of the University of Wyoming football team were dismissed from the team simply for requesting permission to wear black armbands during a game against BYU, as a sign of protest against the LDS Church's ban on Black priesthood holders. The incident drew national attention and sparked controversy (Hamilton 2016).

In response to the protests at BYU, some universities, particularly those with significant Black student populations, refused to schedule athletic competitions with the LDS school. For example, the University of Texas at El Paso canceled a football game with BYU in 1969, Stanford University canceled all athletics against BYU in 1970, and the University of Wyoming canceled a basketball game with BYU in 1971. (*African Americans and the Church of Jesus Christ of Latter-day Saints* 2023)

The LDS Church's policy on race and the priesthood changed in 1978, when Church leaders announced that all worthy male members could hold the priesthood, regardless of race.

Many of the women I interviewed said they had felt the Church was out of step with the progress of civil rights, and the ban on the priesthood was a huge sticking point for them. Justice Durham[2] told me that fighting for civil rights on her college campus was the first time she started to question her faith community, as they stood resolutely against seeing Black people as equal. This caused chafing between her and the Church for more than a full decade before she was finally able to resolve the issue internally. One benefit of that experience: She had learned how to deal with the conflict and colliding of moral authorities (her own and the Church's) surrounding the Black LDS members and the priesthood issue, so when the women's movement gained steam, she already knew how to cope with the disconnect. She had the same experience during the Vietnam War, when an apostle mentioned in a fireside, she attended that those who were against the Vietnam War were like the pacifists in England in 1938, when Hitler was rising to power. She spoke up at the fireside to refute the apostle's statement. Thus, by the time the women's rights movement was at its zenith, she'd already had two social issues with which she had experienced friction within the Church.

"The Decade of the Woman"

The 1970s was the undisputed decade of the woman.[3] Although the Equal Rights Amendment was first drafted in 1923, it wasn't

---

2. Christine Durham Oral Interview, April 23, 2023
3. Eisenstein, Z. (1981). *The radical future of liberal feminism*. Longman; Rosen, R. (2000). *The world split open: How the modern women's movement changed*

until the '70s that the fight for it became a nationwide battle. In 1970, women still couldn't have a credit card or buy a house with a mortgage. Many employers fired women who became pregnant, marital rape and domestic violence were not legal crimes, and no-fault divorce did not exist which limited options for women to extricate themselves from marriages. Educational equality was nonexistent, as many colleges and universities had admissions policies that limited or excluded women from programs or prevented their admission altogether. Scholarship and financial aid were often biased against women: Many scholarships were exclusively available to male students, while others had discriminatory requirements or were limited to specific fields of study considered more "appropriate" for women, such as teaching or nursing. Women faced significant barriers in participating in sports, particularly at the collegiate level. Title IX, a federal law prohibiting sex discrimination in educational institutions that received funding from the federal government, was not passed until 1972. Before that, female athletes had lim-

---

America. Viking; Hanisch, C. (1970). The personal is political. In S. Firestone & A. Koedt (Eds.), *Notes from the second year: Women's liberation*. Radical Feminism; Echols, A. (1989). *Daring to be bad: Radical feminism in America, 1967–1975*. University of Minnesota Press; Dicker, R. (2008). *A history of U.S. feminisms*. Seal Press; Giddings, P. (1984). *When and where I enter: The impact of Black women on race and sex in America*. William Morrow; U.S. National Archives. (n.d.). *The 1970s and Title IX*. https://www.archives.gov/education/lessons/titleix; Horowitz, D. (2000). *Betty Friedan and the making of the feminine mystique: The American left, the cold war, and modern feminism*. University of Massachusetts Press; Brownmiller, S. (1975). *Against our will: Men, women and rape*. Simon & Schuster; MacKinnon, C. A. (1987). *Feminism unmodified: Discourses on life and law*. Harvard University Press.

ited opportunities, fewer resources, and unequal funding compared to male athletes.

As the women's movement became a monumental force that could no longer be ignored, Congress began to enact laws that grappled with some of the challenges women faced in the United States.

Below is a timeline showing the history of policies that affected women and eliminated some of the gender inequality:

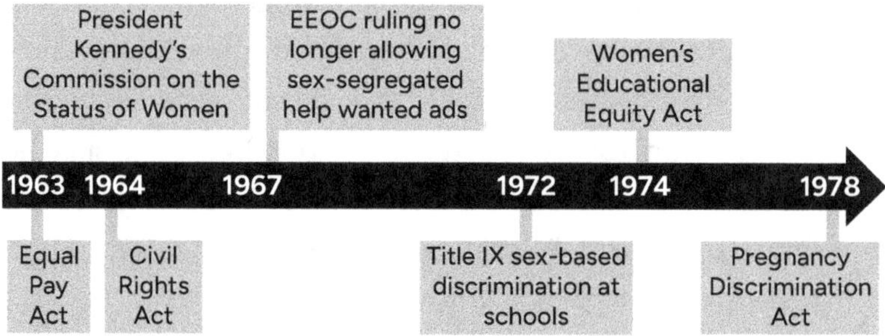

The Equal Rights Amendment (ERA) had been on a slow burn to passage since 1923 when it was first introduced. Congress passed the ERA in May 1972, and it was sent to the States for ratification. With the passage of the Equal Rights Amendment (ERA) in thirty-five of the thirty-eight required states, the typically apolitical LDS Church finally weighed in[4]: It officially opposed the amendment less than a month before it came up

---

4. Prior to the official Frist Presidency Statement in 1976, Then Elder Thomas Monson wrote about the ERA, Thomas S. Monson, "The Women's Movement: Liberation or Deception?," *Ensign*, Jan. 1971, 17–20. The Church had an in-house position statement November 1974 that outlined opposition to the ERA. Barbara Smith, President of the Relief Society was chosen to give a December 1974 address at the LDS Institute in Salt Lake City that outlined opposition to the ERA. An anonymous Editorial in the LDS Church News in

for passage in Utah. With their disapproval transparent, the Church could double down on the narrative in pamphlets, directives, curriculum, and from the pulpit in General Conference that a woman's role was *only* to be a wife and a mother. If the ERA were passed and women joined the work force en masse, the Church warned, the consequences would include the destruction of the family, women would be drafted into the military, all bathrooms would be unisex, gay marriage would be acceptable, and lesbianism would become rampant.

The fight against the Equal Rights Amendment was taken down to the local church level and sometimes hijacked by other conservative groups that wanted the defeat of the ERA.[5] Much has been written[6] about the confusing time where political efforts were intertwined with local church leaders, and conservative groups, which sometimes was perceived as using "the end justifies the means" in the effort to block the ratification of the ERA in the required thirty-eight states. An LDS woman in a hot-

---

January 1975 opposing the ERA were all groundwork laid before the official statement by the First Presidency October 22, 1976 (Bradley 2005)

5. "At a key meeting in Salt Lake City on October 5, 1979, at which selected stake presidents and statewide ERA coordinators were gathered, Elder Hinckley outlined a new method for dealing with political issues He told the group that: 1. People should not be set apart for this work; 2. Should not use LDS in the title of the organizations [but that] 3. church buildings could be used for ERA educations; [and] 4. any and all Church meetings are appropriate forums for discussing ERA; 5. [they] should not use Church funds; [but] 6. Educating members on ERA issues [is appropriate]; 7. [they should] not endorse political candidates—but [should] publish [an] incumbent's voting record." *Pedestals & Podiums, Utah Women, Religious Authority & Equal Rights*, Martha Sonntag Bradley.

6. *Pedestals & Podiums, Utah Women, Religious Authority & Equal Rights*, Martha Sonntag Bradley.

ly contested state had the ERA on her ballot and could expect to see flyers at church that promoted campaign efforts to defeat the amendment, as well as call to actions that involved civic engagement efforts. Much political ire and division within in wards, resulted from this push by members and local leaders of the Church to get involved in the political arena to defeat the ERA.

The push for the defeat of the ERA coincided with the correlated era of the Church, where curriculum as well as communication was handled centrally. With the focus on the women's movement, messaging changed from previous generations. Between 1850–1960, the word *motherhood* was mentioned seventy-four times in General Conference. But between 1960–2020, Church leaders spoke about motherhood 184 times, more than doubling the number of mentions in a little more than half the time.

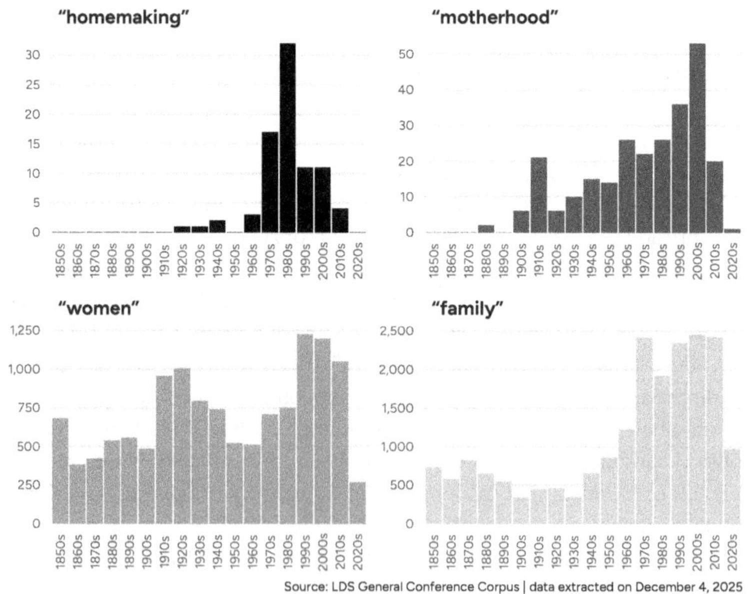

Source: LDS General Conference Corpus | data extracted on December 4, 2025

Early in the LDS Church's history it was seen as very progressive when it came to women's education and civic engagement. The LDS church since its inception has continued to evolve. Over time, many factors including annexation into the United States, the rise of communism and its associated antidote of the strong family propelled the LDS church out of the perceived progressive category to being perceived as extremely conservative. In the Church's own words when explaining its position on the ERA, used the early beginnings as evidence of being for the value of women:

> From its beginnings, The Church of Jesus Christ of Latter-day Saints has affirmed the exalted role of women in our society. . . . In Utah, where our Church is headquartered, women received the right to vote in 1870, fifty years before the Nineteenth Amendment to the Constitution granted them nationally.[7]

In response to the Women's Movement, Church leaders sought to define the role and value of women. In a January 1971 *Ensign* article, "The Women's Movement: Liberation or Deception," then-apostle Thomas S. Monson stated:

> While the motives of its supporters may be praiseworthy, the ERA as a blanket attempt to help women could indeed bring them far more restraints and repressions. We fear it will even

---

7. The right to vote for women, did not apply to Native American or Asian women in Utah.

stifle many God-given feminine instincts. It would strike at the family, humankind's basic institution. The ERA would bring ambiguity and possibly invite extensive litigation. Passage of the ERA, some legal authorities contend, could nullify many accumulated benefits to women in present statutes. We recognize men and women as equally important before the Lord, but with differences biologically, emotionally, and in other ways. The ERA, we believe, does not recognize these differences. There are better means for giving women, and men, the rights they deserve.

Then-prophet President Spencer W. Kimball said this about the role of women:

Too many mothers work away from home to furnish sweaters and music lessons and trips and fun for their children. Too many women spend their time in socializing, in politicking, in public services when they should be home to teach and train and receive and love their children into security.[8]

Numerous divorces can be traced directly to the day when the wife left the home and went out into the world into employment. Two in-

---

8. Spencer W. Kimball, *The Teachings of Spencer W. Kimball* (Salt Lake City: Deseret Book, 1962), 319.

comes raise the standard of living beyond its norm. Two spouses working prevent the complete and proper home life, break into the family prayers, create an independence which is not cooperative, causes distortion, limits the family, and frustrates the children already born.[9]

And President Kimball taught in an Arizona Area Conference in 1977, which was subsequently published in his book Teachings of the Prophet Spencer W Kimball in 1982 and was subsequently quoted by in 1987, Pres. Ezra Taft Benson "To the Mothers in Zion"[10]:

> I beg of you, you who could and should be bearing and rearing a family: wives, come home from the typewriter, the laundry, the nursing, come home from the factory, the café. No career approaches in importance that of wife, homemaker, mother—cooking meals, washing dishes, making beds for one's precious husband and children. Come home, wives, to your husbands. Make home a heaven for them. Come home, wives, to your children, born and unborn. Wrap the motherly cloak about you and, unembarrassed, help in a major role to create the bodies for the immortal souls who anxiously await.[11]

---

9. Spencer W. Kimball, fireside address in San Antonio, Texas, Dec. 3, 1977.
10. Benson, Ezra Taft B, *"To the Mothers in Zion"*, 1987
11. Kimball, *Teachings*, 319.

Church leaders were prescribing a narrow role for women, but it only seemed to apply to white, middle- to upper-middle-class women because of the economic means that were required to fulfill this vision of a women's role. Many faithful women tried to rationalize or justify their own situations in light of these pronouncements from prophets and other General Authorities, and the result was a great deal of friction—both for the women and the general membership of the Church.

Role of Women in the Church

The fight for passage of the ERA coincided with the diminished role of women in the Church. Founded in 1842 by groundbreaking women such as Eliza R. Snow and Emma Hale Smith, the Relief Society gave charitable service and strengthened the female community. The original mission of the Relief Society of The Church of Jesus Christ of Latter-day Saints was to provide support, charity, and spiritual growth for women within the Church and in the communities where they dwelt. Led by strong female leaders, the Relief Society aimed to foster a sense of sisterhood, empower women, and promote service to others. The goals of the Relief Society were multifaceted, encompassing both temporal and spiritual aspects. Women were encouraged to seek knowledge and education, develop their talents, and care for the needy. The Relief Society originally had its own budget and curriculum, and its "general president," as she was called, ran the organization.

In 1970, however, the Church consolidated the structure under the Priesthood Correlation Department, and the Relief

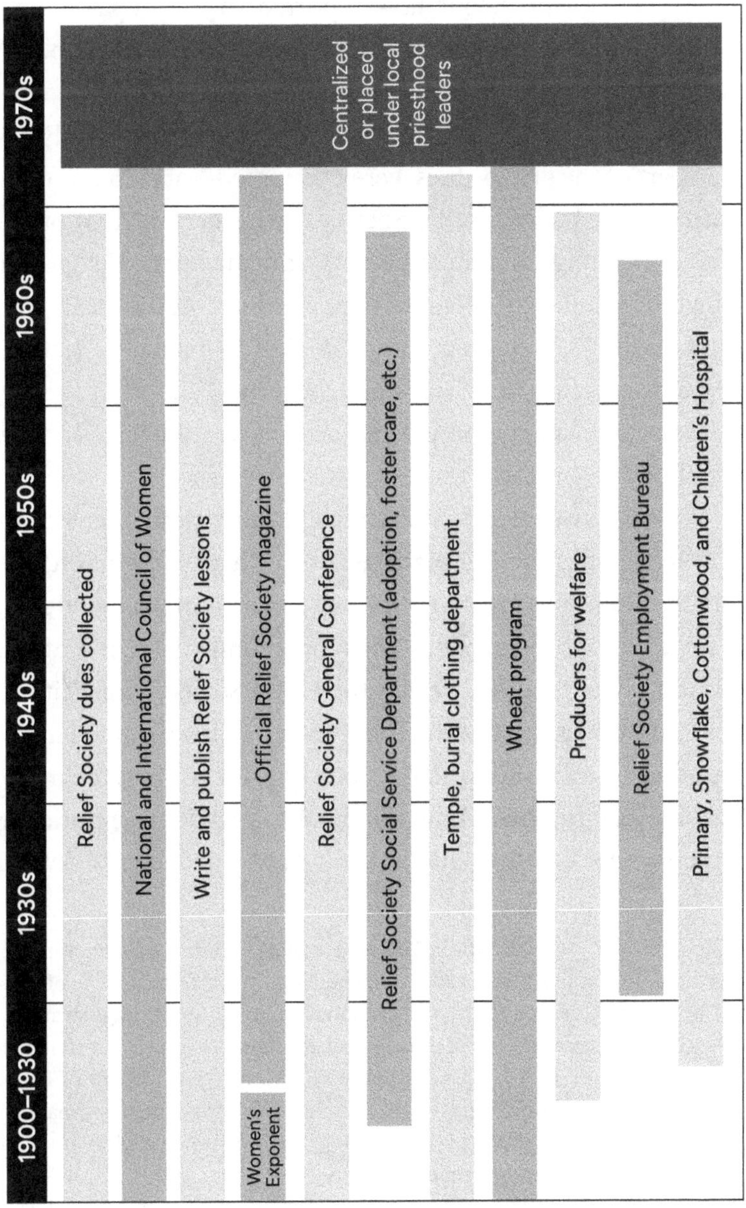

1900–1930
1930s
1940s
1950s
1960s
1970s
Relief Society dues collected
National and International Council of Women
Write and publish Relief Society lessons
Women's Exponent
Official Relief Society magazine
Relief Society General Conference
Relief Society Social Service Department (adoption, foster care, etc.)
Temple, burial clothing department
Wheat program
Producers for welfare
Relief Society Employment Bureau
Primary, Snowflake, Cottonwood, and Children's Hospital
Centralized or placed under local priesthood leaders

Society general president now reported to the department's managing director. The Relief Society had long been an "opt-in" organization to which women paid dues, but during the consolidation all LDS women eighteen and older automatically became part of the group, dues were eliminated—and so was their control of the budget. Relief Society classes became part of the block of meetings on Sunday, and the organization was forever changed, including leadership opportunities. Additionally, the Relief Society's long-held responsibility of managing welfare programs such as the Wheat Fund, hospitals, adoption agency, social services, and employment bureau was transferred to the Priesthood organization.[12]

With the movement to centralize all activities under Priesthood leadership for the management of a global church, the women's ability to create their own curriculum was hindered, as it had to go through a long chain of command in correlation. This laborious process affected the Relief Society's capacity to speak on women's rights and roles.[13] Many of the women I interviewed were involved in Relief Society prior to these changes, and they saw firsthand how the outside world was embracing women while the LDS Church seemed to be pedaling backward

---

12. Relief Society Organization Timeline Relief Society Organization Research Guide. (2023). Retrieved from The Church Of Jesus Christ of Latter-Day Saints: https://history.churchofjesuschrist.org/training/library/relief-society-organization-research-guide/relief-society-organization-timeline
13. Saints, T. C.-D. (n.d.). IMPORTANT EVENTS IN THE History of Relief Society. Retrieved from https://www.churchofjesuschrist.org/study/manual/daughters-in-my-kingdom-the-history-and-work-of-relief-society/important-events-in-the-history-of-relief-society
The Nineteenth Amendment to the Constitution granted them nationally.

in the area of women's rights. The women felt disempowered and discouraged.

Because of these constant messages within the LDS faith community, a division arose between women who worked outside the home and women who stayed home. Most LDS women in the United States, whether they worked or didn't, felt the discord.

Unfortunately, all this turmoil around race and women's rights were coming to a head just when the women I interviewed were making their "and" decisions—being a mother *and* something else. They felt an uncomfortable dissonance between their own moral authority and the Church's pronouncements on these issues.

Ultimately while this dissonance was uncomfortable and at times created hurt feelings or offense on all sides, it led to opportunities for the women I interviewed to dig deep and reconcile for themselves what God felt about them and their chosen paths.

Why This
Resonates With Me

My Own Story

||||||||||||||||||||||||||||||

I'm not sure how someone like me, who doesn't like to write and doesn't dream of being an author, ends up writing a book. As I look back on my life to this point, this is a pattern I keep following: I do something I don't want to, that I've never dreamed of doing, just because I feel compelled to do it.

I recently did a rebranding exercise for myself and asked for feedback from people who have worked with me. What surprised me was that the qualities and strengths they identified all came because of a pattern that has become so prevalent in my life: doing what I know to be my path instead of doing what *I* want to do. I asked colleagues what words came to mind when they thought of me, and collectively they said: fearless, fast, innovative, formidable, smart, collaborative, and leader. When asked to describe my personality, collectively they said: outgoing, quick to laugh, always in motion/making things happen, kind, invested in the success of the people around her, does not suffer fools, woman of faith and inclusive.

Obviously, all the characteristics they listed have double-edged swords. One of my defining traits, which nobody else seems to recognize but leads to what everyone can see on the outside, is my ability to dwell comfortably in ambiguity. I don't need certainty. I can easily hold two competing ideas that might both be true and not let the friction between them slow me down; on the contrary, the friction propels me forward. That's the result of following courses I didn't initiate myself.

I grew up outside Seattle, Washington, where we had beautiful trails, the ocean and lakes, and an innovative way of thinking. My dad was an avid sportsman who taught my two sisters and me how to play many sports. He instilled in us the belief that we had no barriers just because we were girls—he was ahead of his time with his motto, "You can do anything as a woman."

My parents were raised very differently. My mother's mother was an inactive member of the Church, and her father was not religious. My mother sought out religion in ninth grade, when her family moved to Cape Canaveral, Florida, for her father's job transfer with Boeing. She had decided she was going to start attending meetings at the LDS Church, which she had been exposed to on her visits to her maternal grandmother's house in Idaho. She attended without her parents and decided to go to BYU when she graduated. She met my dad in Seattle after her graduation from college.

My father grew up in a deeply religious Catholic home. He went to parochial schools and thought he would join the priesthood someday. (One of his boyhood friends is actually serving in the Vatican today.) When I was growing up, my dad attended the 7:30 a.m. Sunday mass at Holy Family Catholic Church down the street from our house, while my mother attended the LDS ward that was also close by. As children, we were given the opportunity to attend both services, and we would alternate between the two. I liked the LDS Church better because of Primary. The Catholic church was all quiet and we weren't allowed to make much noise during Mass, whereas at the LDS Church there was always chaos. I never understood why Catholic families were able to be quiet during the service and yet LDS families couldn't.

We didn't discuss anything religious or spiritual in our home, I think because my parents disagreed on their outlook. I do remember my dad having issues with the LDS Church about women, because he had three daughters and he believed we could do anything, and he felt that the LDS Church didn't treat us that way.

I was told in Primary that if you read the Book of Mormon and prayed about it, you would know it was true. At eight years old, I just assumed everyone in the Church was doing this, so I read the whole book. I prayed about it and had an experience that—just as I assumed would happen—confirmed the truthfulness of the book, and I decided to be baptized in the LDS faith. It wasn't until I was about seventeen years old that I learned that my experience that confirmed the Book of Mormon's veracity was not typical. I naively assumed everyone had irrefutable experiences with the Divine that confirmed its truthfulness. Having this experience at such a young age guided my choices but also solidified for me that God was real and that

He heard my prayers, and that gave me what I needed to be able to move forward. My experience with receiving an answer gave me self-confidence from an early age that religion was a deeply personal thing and that personal revelation was the keystone.

I remember having other experiences that fortified this ability to hold two competing ideas in my heart and reconcile them. I remember sitting in a Young Women's class, where back in the day there were seven lessons on marriage a year and only one on Christ. I know this because I later had to teach those same lessons. Because I was from the maligned "part-member family," the lessons hit me differently. My advisors would be talking about eternal marriage and tell these stories from the Young Women's manual about Nancy who went out with a NONMEMBER, and before you know it, she became addicted to hashish and eventually became a prostitute—all because she dated a nonmember. I would hear these stories and physically look around the room at the small group of LDS youth and think, *Are you kidding? My family is more functional than all of you with your "eternal marriages."* Whenever they would imply that "nonmembers" were not as good, my entire body and intellect would revolt. I learned to listen to that revolt in my body as a gauge for truth. I was able to see the good in people, whether they were Catholic, LDS, Buddhist, Muslim, or atheist.

Because we were a part-member family, we were not really a part of the social gathering of our ward. This was a huge blessing for me in my life. Because I went to church to worship, not for social community, I could distinguish between the two: church was for worship, the community was for service. Church was not a place where I tried to "fit in."

By the time I was sixteen, I knew I was good at business. I wanted to get a finance degree, work for two years, then get an MBA. I never planned on going to BYU—my dad and I both thought it wasn't academically rigorous—but I applied as a backup. I remember knowing deep down that I *should* go to BYU, but I didn't want to. This internal conflict gave me a stomachache for months. My high school counselor eventually called me in at the end of April and told me I had to declare where I was going by May 1. I finally faced the stomachache and God and declared for BYU. My stomachache went away, and I have always remembered that my body and my eternal spirit knew what was best for me.

At BYU, I was in the finance department at a time when there were hardly any females there. I recently checked, and BYU still doesn't have a strong representation of females in finance. For the first time in my life, I ran into the narrative that women couldn't do whatever they wanted. I had been shielded from this mindset because of my family and where I grew up. I remember having male BYU finance students tell me that I was taking the spot of a breadwinner—which left me dumbfounded. Of course, I responded with my characteristic directness and none of the grace I wish I'd had at that age: "Of course I'm not taking up their spot! If they were as smart as I am, they would have had this spot."

When I look back on my life, there have been quite a few of those moments where *I knew* God wanted me to do something that wasn't what *I* wanted to do. I became adept at recognizing those moments, and that has created who I am. For example, I had it when I decided to serve a mission for The

Church of Jesus Christ of Latter-day Saints. Before then, it had never occurred to me to go on a mission. The missionaries never stopped by our house growing up; I don't know if my parents requested them not to come, or if they didn't see the value of visiting part-member families. In any event, I had no exposure to them at all. I also had a plan: I was graduating, working, then getting an MBA. Why would I go on a mission? However, at BYU, people started asking me if I was going on a mission. I was incredulous—of course I wasn't! But being the rational person I am, I decided I would fast about it, so then I could tell people I had fasted and prayed about it and didn't have to go.

Again, an unmistakable experience happened as I fasted, and I knew I had to go. I had no idea how to make this work, as my dad was Catholic and wouldn't support a mission, and I had not saved any money for it. I remember calling my parents and telling them I was going on a mission as soon as the semester was over, and I needed my parents to pay for it. My dad curtly said, "No," and hung up the phone. I didn't hear from them for a week. He finally called me back and said, "OK, you can go on a mission if you graduate first." (In our family, education was the number-one priority.) I told him, "Oh no, I have to go now. I'm *supposed* to go now."

They wanted to think about it. When they got back to me (and I have no idea what discussion they had in Seattle), they said that if I left at the end of the semester, so that I would miss the least amount of school possible, they would support me. To my dad's credit, he wrote me a letter every week on my mission and talked about the apostle Paul in his letters. My mission was extremely strict about communication with family, so we weren't able to call home at all during those eighteen months, not even Christmas or Mother's Day. This was quite a trial for my mom and my Catholic dad, but he supported me no matter what.

When I left on my mission, I brought with me my conviction that the Book of Mormon was key to my communication with God, but my mission experiences and years at BYU taught me how to live in a community with differing worldviews and perspectives. Both BYU and my mission gave me insight into the Church in a way I wouldn't have gotten anywhere else.

After graduate school, my plan was to stay in Seattle to continue working for a major tech company there. However, Intel in Portland flew me down there for an interview, and the minute I walked off the plane I knew I was supposed to go there. However, knowing and doing are two different things. I had a stomachache for months, and every time Intel called to negotiate with me, I was "conveniently" not around (this was before cell phones). I would call them back, but always after hours and leave a voice message. (Just a little background: Seattle natives know that Seattle is better in every way than Portland. Our city is bigger, it's surrounded by water on all sides, and my friends, family, and then-boyfriend were all there.) The tech company I was working for was a better company than Intel and it didn't make sense, rationally, to move to Oregon. But as I had learned and would continue to learn, rational strategic decisions don't always line up with what God has in mind. I finally decided I would do what God wanted, but I asked Intel to up the offer by four times on the stock options and the cash bonus. I rationalized that if they rejected my requests, I could say that I had done what God wanted by being willing to go. To my great surprise, Intel agreed to my request, and I accepted the offer to work in Oregon. My stomachache immediately went away.

I remember always feeling that as a woman in the high-tech industry, I had to prove I was as smart as (or smarter than) the men and that I could do whatever I set my mind to. But one day when I was almost thirty, I realized I had already demonstrated that. I had been successful in every part of my career. I had this existential moment where I realized *nobody* viewed me as inferior—nobody believed it was a competition. It was more about me believing it. That moment freed me from any expectations of others, and I have been taking risks and failing ever since. Through all that, I learned to be pretty fearless, and a big reason for that is that I'm not afraid to fail.

I've continued throughout my life to have experiences where the strategic mind that has made me successful in my career came in direct conflict with what God wanted me to do. I came to rely on those experiences where my body (stomachaches) became the truth barometer.

Just like the women I interviewed, I found that there was not only friction in my career but also within my own faith community. Besides the obvious clash with women pursuing a full-time career, I also felt the friction between the narrative I gleaned from the scriptures about being like Christ, where there was no mention of Christ having a family, and the Church community being all about the eternal family.

I had a few life-altering experiences that taught me that Christ really does see us on an individual level, and personal revelation is the key to developing our growth as individuals. The stories of the women I interviewed resonated with me when they talked about their own beliefs formed from their experience with Divinity and how sometimes those didn't completely line up with what they heard in church. That was my experience as well. I had some amazing conversations with local priesthood leaders who supported and listened to me, but there were also times when they didn't. Those experiences helped me wrestle with my questions about the purpose of the Church. What is my role when my own personal experience and revelation are belittled? How do I continue to grow from the friction I experience, instead of decelerating?

I have had other painful interactions with people in this community, and I have had my own personal revelations and experiences that have made me want to weep. However, these experiences have made me who I am and have taught me invaluable lessons. These experiences taught me that sometimes, those in positions of power get it wrong, and God will let you know when they do. I learned that it's God's Church, and it's *His* job to fix it if He chooses, not mine. My job is to learn and grow as much as I can as I draw closer to my Savior, getting as much light as I can. As a result of engaging in the Church and letting my own revelation guide me, I was able to excavate a crater in my heart.

I can see the gaps in our collective knowledge, but that doesn't frighten me. It actually gives me a sense of grace—I believe that the more we don't know, the more it's OK to fail and to fail fast. That's one of the hallmarks of my life: I'm able to hold the ambiguity, move forward with personal revelation, and learn from the community as I serve in it.

There are things I still don't understand, but that doesn't make them any less real. For instance, I have had the privilege of having ancestors show up at the temple when their work is being done. This is how I know that there is something real about the ordinances that I don't understand—that somehow, doing a ritual in our mortal bodies connects our eternal spirit and Heaven all together and eliminates time just for a moment, and brings us closer to Christ. Somehow, we have these essential ordinances, and we have the authority to perform them. For that, I'm very grateful.

Something Anne Osborn said in our interview really resonated with me. Like her, I have known truth throughout my life. When I've known it, I have stuck to it, regardless of those around me and their narratives. I know Christ lives. I know the Book of Mormon testifies of Him. I know these truths because of personal study and revelation, and I will continue to stick to it.

Organizations Set Up for Friction

Kathleen Flake

When I embarked on this project, my initial vision was to compile narratives about remarkable women navigating a period of societal upheaval and transformation. As I delved into their stories, however, a central theme emerged: friction. As defined in physics, friction is the force that opposes the motion of an object, causing it to lose energy and slow down. Without friction, a sled pushed across the snow would continue moving indefinitely after being propelled.

These women not only encountered friction in the world along their life paths, but they also faced resistance within their faith communities. What's fascinating about friction is its innate neutrality—it is neither inherently good nor bad. While I'm no physicist, I know that interpreting the world through the lens of friction challenges conventional notions of conflict and right versus wrong. Friction simply exists; it's how we harness it that makes a difference.

Friction is an integral part of our daily lives. Without it, we wouldn't be able to walk or pick up objects. Take slipping on a slippery path, for example—without friction, we can't control our steps. Even muscle-building relies on friction, as resistance triggers muscle growth. Friction increases as we slow down, so the more we slow our progress, the more friction we encounter. Additionally, the heavier the weight of a moving body on a surface, the stronger the force of friction. This is a physical law, but it can also be metaphorically applied to human pursuits: Those who undertake significant tasks or responsibilities inevitably face more friction.

The women I interviewed forged new paths and shouldered substantial responsibilities, and consequently encountered amplified resistance. They were acutely aware of the resistance friction, but what mattered was their response to it. Did they allow it to slow them down, increasing the actual friction until they came to a halt? Ultimately, too much friction—if you allow it—will immobilize you.

Another intriguing aspect of friction is its relationship with surface roughness. The rougher the surfaces in contact, the higher the friction. Smooth surfaces obviously generate less drag. From a gospel perspective, this scientific law offers a profound metaphor. As we smooth our "rough edges," we encounter less friction not only with other "smooth" (godlike) beings but also with other "rough" (human) beings.

By virtue of their innovative approaches, pioneers often face an additional layer of chafing. Many of the women I interviewed were trailblazers in their fields, and their very novelty invited resistance. Their faith communities, too, contributed to this friction, but these women refused to let it derail their unique journeys. They confronted it head-on, resolved to overcome it and achieve their goals.

When it came to friction within their faith communities, each woman had her own way of dealing with it. For each of them, the decision ultimately boiled down to calculating the return on investment (ROI) of remaining in an organization that presented friction. The stories that follow highlight the various types of resistance these women faced and the strategies they used to circumnavigate it. The lesson we can learn from them is that friction can lead to growth, and that, ultimately, is why we are on this earth: to grow. Friction will always exist in any organization, so how do we recognize, with open eyes and hearts, when the benefits of staying in an organization outweigh the abrasion it causes? How do we decide to stay for the growth opportunity it presents?

The rest of the book delves into the various kinds of resistance we encounter and why we choose to stay despite and sometimes because of it. Through my research, I discovered that each person has different ways of calculating their ROI within their faith community. It became clear that people have diverse foundational reasons for staying, depending on how they value different aspects of their religion. For instance, a friend of mine stays in the LDS Church because she knows her entire ward will show up at her funeral. She sees this loyal sense of community as a benefit of being a participating member of the Church.

In general, each woman I interviewed recognized the friction their faith communities created with regard to women's roles and racial inequality. They were well aware of the disparity between their own perspectives and desires and the official narratives of the LDS Church. They didn't turn a blind eye to the friction but rather sought to reconcile their feelings, impressions, and aspirations with the faith community's narrative. Through this process, they were able to circumnavigate the friction and remain active members of the Church. They didn't try to confront the entire organization to dispel the friction; instead, they focused on the aspects they could influence while living authentic lives true to their beliefs.

My conclusions about friction crystallized during my conversation with Kathleen Flake, a historian and scholar who has dedicated her life to studying the influence of law on American religion and the impact of the First Amendment religious clauses. Currently the Richard Lyman Bushman Chair of Mormon Studies at the University of Virginia, Kathleen shed light on the notion of "competing moralities." Instead of asking how she could stay in the faith community when her positions conflicted with the official narratives, she reframed it as a question of navigating conflicting principles.[1]

Kathleen and I discussed how organizations establish boundaries along ideological and community lines, and how religion is a perfect example of those lines of demarcation. As I contemplated this new paradigm, it became evident that friction arises when we encounter these boundaries. Kathleen pointed out that while we often expect religion to be safe for people, in practice and academia there is a fundamental un-

---

1. (Flake 2023)

derstanding that we cannot make institutions safe for people. Rather, we can only make people safe for institutions. This resonated with me, although I am still grappling with the idea. As we explore how these women were able to stay and thrive in the Church without completely aligning with prevailing narratives, I hope it will become clearer how our reaction to friction along our unique paths can make us safer within the organization.

Personally, my initial response to boundaries has been to break them down, thus eliminating the friction. But if we believe that our purpose on this earth is to grow, we can't allow our reaction to friction to slow us to a stop. After all, we know there is an "opposition in all things." The expression "the organization is perfect but the people within it aren't" feels less accurate, when I consider that organizations are intentionally designed to have boundaries and create friction.

During the 1970s, amidst the debate over ERA, Kathleen Flake co-wrote a pamphlet titled "Mormons for ERA." She remains an advocate for women's equality and believes that God values men and women equally. However, with the passage of fifty years, Kathleen now contemplates the ERA issue from a more introspective perspective. What if the prophet had received an answer to fight against the ERA? What if there are now sound legal issues that couldn't have been foreseen in the 1970s that shed a different perspective on what passage of that specific wording of the law would have meant? Like many personal revelations we receive, we are often given only a piece or pieces of the puzzle, and it is up to us and our worldview to implement the answer we receive. The nuanced view she is able to see is that maybe the friction came with the imperfect implementation of the prompting. Those who fought the ERA, for example, had a worldview shaped by the culture of the 1950s, predominantly composed of white, middle- to upper-middle-class Americans. The official Church narratives for women were aligned with the societal norms of that time. However, the denunciation against working outside the home applied to all LDS women, creating friction not only for those who felt their path included working outside the home but also for those who lived outside the United States or were lower class or non-white, where the practical needs or cultural norms didn't already apply. This book showcases what some women did when faced with this conflict.

Kathleen and I also discussed the statement, "The Church is true." Grammatically, I have always struggled with that statement because "the Church" is a noun. It is like saying, "This blue shirt is true." Kathleen posed a better question: What do we mean when we say, "I know the Church is true"? She suggests we ask whether the gospel according to the LDS Church is real for us. Is it true enough to its mission to act as an instrument for accessing the Divine and making it present and real, helping us know that God is real? Also, apropos of "I know," as we use that phrase with regard to truth, assertions or testimonies of such are always most convincing when used in relation to an experience. Latter-day Saints are, in essence, recapitulating the story of Joseph Smith. Or, to use the Book of Mormon's promise, they have learned that God will "manifest the truth of it." And, when the "it" is made manifest, friction is also reduced by knowing what matters most.

Kathleen used the friction of competing moralities which caused friction to be able to hone in on what was most real and foundational. Kathleen concluded by saying, "I know God is real, and I know that because of the Church."

Search for Answers

Jill Mulvay Derr

|||||||||||||||||||||||||||||||

Jill Mulvay Derr had something of a front-row seat to much of the friction in the Church in the 1970s, and that perspective enabled and informed her studies of Latter-day Saint women. She grew up in Salt Lake City but moved to Boston for graduate school in 1970, which intensified her exposure to conflicts in the United States surrounding civil rights, the Vietnam War, and women's rights. She returned to Utah to work in the Church Historical Department, where she devoted her efforts to studying women in the Church. She became Associate Professor of Church History at Brigham Young University and served as director of BYU's Joseph Fielding Smith Institute for Latter-day Saint History. From 1998–1999, she was also president of the Mormon History Association. Her experiences working within the Church and focusing on women's history have given her a unique perspective on friction and how to use it to move forward in life.

Jill graduated from the University of Utah in 1970 with a bachelor's degree in English, then headed to Boston to study at the Harvard Graduate School of Education to earn her master's degree in teaching. She remained in Boston for a few years to teach middle school students.

Boston in the '70s was home to a unique, vibrant community of LDS women, where individuals from diverse backgrounds and with varying viewpoints came together to engage in meaningful discussions about women's issues. Despite their differences, these women were able to create an environment that fostered understanding, collaboration, and progress. They courageously addressed their concerns, openly discussed pressing issues, and actively sought common ground. Many of the women I interviewed took part in these discussions and found that having a community of women was vital in working out how to deal with friction.

While Jill was involved in a student ward at that time and was acquainted with the Boston women's meetings, she recalled attending a lecture that the group had hosted that became a pivotal moment in her life. Maureen Ursenbach Beecher, an editor for the newly organized History Division at the Church Historical Department, spoke to the group about her research on Eliza R. Snow, and Jill was amazed[1].

"It was stunning to me," Jill told Cherry B. Silver in an interview for BYU Studies. "I had no idea that this person, Eliza R. Snow, had been such a prominent, accomplished figure. I was blown away. I remember asking Maureen, 'How did you find all

---

1. *Fifty Years of Exponent II*, Signature Books

this out?' She talked about her work in the History Division, and that was essentially that."[2]

Jill had planned on returning to Salt Lake to teach, but upon moving to Utah, an associate of hers from Cambridge told her about an internship opportunity in the Church Historical Department. Her initial assignment was to work under Maureen's direction collecting Eliza R. Snow's poetry, so she read her two volumes of poetry and then searched old issues of the *Woman's Exponent,* the *Deseret News,* and the *Juvenile Instructor.* Years later, Jill worked with her colleague Karen Lynn Davidson to turn this research into a book: *Eliza R. Snow: The Complete Poetry.*

Jill worked full-time in the Church Historical Department until 1977, when she married C. Brooklyn Derr.

"After we married, I worked primarily part-time, and that worked well for me," she said. "I started a program for a master's at the University of Utah in American Studies, and I gave it up. We had custody of Brooke's son to start with, and we later got custody of his two daughters, and we had a son of our own, and even though many women could handle all of that, I could see that I could not."

While Jill said she would have liked to finish her degree, she's happy with the work she accomplished both in and outside of the home.

"I really do envy women with families who went on and got PhDs," Jill said. "And I still feel a little inadequate, to be honest with you. But that's part of our tendency to compare, I recognize that. I also feel I can take full responsibility for the

---

2. (Silver 2021)

choices I made, and due to the grace of God, they worked out pretty well."

Jill continued to work at the Church Historical Department until her son was born, after which she worked on contract on books and other publications on women in Church history, such as *Women's Voices: An Untold History of the Latter-day Saints* and *Women of the Covenant: The Story of Relief Society*. She later taught as a professor of Church history at Brigham Young University.

In 1987, President Ezra Taft Benson reiterated President Kimball's 1977 charge for women to not work, and Jill went for validation to Heaven for her course.

"I wanted to work, and I did work, and I can't say I ever felt guilty about it," she said. "I thought what President Benson said required that I really give it some thought and prayer if I was going to continue working. And once I did that, it just wasn't an issue for me. I mean, I felt that I should continue."

One key takeaway I've learned from talking to all the women I've interviewed is that even though your path might not follow what you heard in General Conference, praying and receiving personal revelation for your own course gives you self-confidence: you know that the path you are on is God's path for you.

Because of Jill's unique perch during the 1970s, she has a particular viewpoint on how outside forces in the broader American culture collided with structural changes in the Church as well as its doctrine and culture. Jill acknowledged that some of the greatest friction she felt stemmed from the correlation movement, which was a push to unify the structure and budget of the separate organizations within the Church. Before then, the Relief Society ran a number of welfare organizations and other programs within the Church, the Primary directed Primary Children's Hospital in Salt Lake, and both organizations published their own magazines. After the correlation, those magazines were terminated and replaced by the *Ensign, Liahona,* and *Friend,* and women's major responsibilities were subsumed by departments headed by men.

In an interview with the LDS Women's Project, Jill said, "That was a huge change for Latter-day Saint women. It required a considerable loss of autonomy but reflected the need for the simplification and central direction that enabled internationalization and the growth of a worldwide church. Relief Societies in Utah could have bazaars and fund their projects and decorate their rooms how they wanted. In the Philippines, however, Relief Society women had no resources and no money. They could do much more by being under a ward budget."[3]

Jill's comments reflect the nuance of the situation. While these adjustments made the Church more unified and paved the way for worldwide growth, the changes also represented a loss to many women in the Church because they no longer had the same responsibility or autonomy.

In her interview with the LDS Women's Project, Jill added that these changes in the Church organization were occurring at the same time as dramatic changes for women in the world, and the clash between them caused some dissonance.

"In the world, there was emphasis on women's equality, the Equal Rights Amendment, equal pay for equal work, advanced positions and responsibilities for working women, ex-

---

3. (The liberation of being myself 2021)

panding women's lives into the public sphere, moving beyond the private sphere," Jill said. "At the same time, in the Church there was new emphasis and a real focus on the home, Family Home Evening, priesthood-directed homes, priesthood-directed—usually male-directed—everything, and women's responsibilities in the Church became more narrowly focused on the home."

I asked Jill how she was able to reconcile some of this conflict, and she answered that she did so by challenging the roles she was expected to fulfill. Many people cut her a lot of slack for working outside the home, perhaps because she worked for the Church, and she gleaned a lot from her historical studies that helped assuage the friction she felt. She pointed to other women in the Church during that time who did similar things, like Laurel Thatcher Ulrich, and said they helped erode the set expectations for women in the Church and make room for more diversity.

Jill was also able to differentiate between the perfect and the imperfect within the Church. The Restoration is ongoing, and Jill said her understanding of that meant that she didn't expect perfection from the Church or its members. In her work for the Church Historical Department, she encountered stories and information that was upsetting, but she learned to look at people with a nuanced understanding and accept their flaws.

"I mean, I love Emma Smith, but she's not always the person I want her to be; I see her weaknesses and flaws," Jill told me. "I love Brigham Young, but I can see his flaws."

Jill said that while she does have faith in her community and the fellowship the Church brings, her main testimony lies in her faith in Christ and that this is His restored church and His way of doing things through imperfect beings.

"The imperfections bother me, they hurt, and I recognize that sometimes they hurt people," she said. "On the other hand, I see the larger enterprise as being one for good."

Jill's study of Church history also taught her to see how others in the past had handled friction, and she learned to apply it to her situation.

"Other historians and I felt like one of the women in the nineteenth century, Sarah M. Kimball, who was a close friend of Eliza R. Snow and president of the 15th Ward," Jill said. "When Sarah talked about the suffrage movement in her era, she made a statement that was just how we felt as time went on: 'We were very careful.' And I think that characterized my own work. I was very careful."

Jill explained that the early sisters, including Eliza, were worried that the Relief Society would get shut down again. Brigham Young had previously disbanded it in 1845 because of infighting and his criticism of Emma's opposition to plural marriage and the Twelve, so the women were very careful about how they approached conflict with male priesthood leaders. Jill took a page from that and was very careful in her own dealings within the Church organizational structure, decades after Sarah and Emma's struggles. The examples of those pioneer women of the early Church resonated with Jill and gave her strength to handle friction in a peaceful way.

"I have to say, studying history and seeing the way that Eliza R. Snow, Mary Isabella Horne, Bathsheba Smith, and Zina Young viewed the priesthood and asserted their personal connection to the priesthood authority and power was really affirming for me," she said.

Jill added that being careful is not the same as being motionless.

"There's this continual pushing, and I guess that's how I would characterize my work: trying to push the boundaries, extend the boundaries, without overstepping them," she said. "Part of that I learned from those nineteenth century women . . . Eliza was politically savvy, and she knew where those boundaries were, and the other women did too, and so there was always respect. I feel we can work most effectively within the Church order; we know that we respect the men who lead this church, even if we disagree with them. And we do not publicly confront them, like Emma did. She taught us that there is a high price to pay for open confrontation and we risk losing what we have, and it may take years to rebuild."

Jill said that the kind of pushing women do within the Church is gradual but effective, and it often works best when there is additional pressure from forces without the Church. She noted for example, that the *Woman's Exponent* was only semi-official in its day, and *Exponent II* today serves as an unofficial forum for women's expression and discussion.

"They give themselves rein, so to speak, to have diversity of opinions, because they're not officially [speaking] for the Church," she said. "There are boundaries that you respect, and I think my colleagues and I in the Church Historical Department and at BYU in our own way worked hard to push those boundaries by documenting some sensitive issues, such as women healing the sick. Often, however, pushing from the inside is sometimes invisible. I think it takes both pushing from the inside and from the outside for change to happen."

Jill changed what she could in her sphere of influence. For her, "pushing boundaries" looked like asking questions and thinking critically. She didn't back off from opportunities to educate others or raise her concerns when she felt it was necessary.

"I can't tell you how many times I sat through the old temple endowment ceremony and said to myself, *This is wrong. This is not right. This is not the full story. And I know that someday this will be changed. I know because in my relationship with the Lord, I know this is not right,*" she told me. "So, when I went in for my temple recommend interview with the bishop, I would always say, 'I have a hard time with this part of the temple ritual. And that's hard for me.'"

Jill spoke to me about her love of ritual within the Church and said that she appreciated attending to the temple and especially serving as an ordinance worker. She believes, in a way we don't understand, rituals help us break the time continuum we are in on Earth and for a moment we can connect with the Divine. Our mortal bodies can connect with our eternal spirits and, in a way, we can touch Heaven. However, Jill felt a disconnect between her appreciation for the temple rituals and some aspects of them that she felt were incomplete or incorrect.

She spoke with multiple temple presidents about her questions and concerns, and she said she was able to feel peace despite the frustration she felt because she knew that there was a bigger picture that she simply couldn't see yet. Although over time, numerous adjustments have been made to temple ceremonies, Jill remembers the very day in 2019 when further changes were announced. She and her husband were then serving as ordinance workers in the Salt Lake Temple.

"The day in 2019 that changes were introduced," Jill recalled. "It was like beams of light raining down on these women ordinance workers—old, young, everyone was just rejoicing. It was such a happy moment."

Jill said that she has moments where she talks to women in the Church who say that the changes aren't enough.

"I'm thinking, *Wait a minute. Do you know that I waited forty years for these changes? Can you not wait another little while to see what else changes?* We're learning as a community, line upon line."

Waiting four decades is hard but change within an organization is always harder than individual change. It takes time. Within each one of our spheres of influence, we can ask questions to get better educated and spark more understanding in others and encourage positive evolution. Jill was a master of this; throughout her life, she has made an effort to educate herself and others. She recalled how a former bishop would always "thank the Aaronic Priesthood" for passing the Sacrament, and she explained to him privately that the men were priesthood holders rather than the priesthood itself and asked him to change his wording accordingly.

"I must have talked to him for five minutes, and he could not understand what I was saying," Jill said. "And I think that is part of the issue, where you see these pockets of people who don't understand. And in part, they're the people who grew up in a correlated Church that was more top-down."

Jill said that although it may be frustrating or difficult to challenge old beliefs and practices and teach those who hold them, it is always worth it to try.

"It's good to have questions," she told me. "It's a good thing to search for the answers. The whole idea that there should be no questions is counterintuitive."

Jill opened up my eyes to so many facets of how I can use friction to move forward in my life instead of letting it slow me down. Things do change, and Jill shows that we can be part of the change we'd like to see in our communities by pushing, little by little, until we erode the boundaries set for us.

Offense and Healing

Dr. Elizabeth Hammond

||||||||||||||||||||||||||||||||

Dr. Mary Elizabeth Hale Hammond, an innovative anatomic pathologist, has faced friction in both her career and her faith community because of her dedication to challenging conventional wisdom and the status quo.

At a time when few women attended medical school, Elizabeth pushed past prejudice and discrimination to graduate at the top of her class from the University of Utah School of Medicine in 1967. The author of 190 published manuscripts and three books, she has played a pivotal role in creating education programs for pathologists, especially in molecular testing of breast cancer. One of her most important contributions to research was her discovery of a long-overlooked protein that causes rejection of organ transplants.

Elizabeth is jubilant and extremely articulate, and I learned a lot from my conversation with her. She brought home the idea that friction arises when you are an innovator, whether in your chosen career or in your faith community. Her greatest scientific breakthrough stalled for over a decade because others in her field did not see what she could see. She was a challenger, while people around her looked at things the way they had always been.

In her spiritual life, Elizabeth has also had a unique journey. When I met with her, she told me that personal revelation was essential to her faith. Over the years, she has also found that forgiveness and repentance are the keys to keeping the heavens open for revelation.

Elizabeth credits her parents with supporting her ambition as soon as she decided, in the eighth grade, that she wanted to become a doctor.

"Nobody in my family thought that was crazy, even though at the time, medicine was not a typical path for a woman," she told me. "My parents said, 'OK, well, let's find out what you have to do to become a doctor.' My father took me to the University of Utah, we got a list of classes I would need to take if I wanted to study medicine, and I just went down that path."[1]

Her decision was met with opposition from all sides. People in her neighborhood and extended family made snide remarks and suggested that she would be better off quitting school.

"My aunts were constantly badgering my mother about me and my educational choices," Elizabeth recalled. She said they would ask, "Why aren't you just happy getting married and having babies?'"

Elizabeth graduated high school in 1960 and attended the University of Utah for three years to complete her undergrad-

---

1. (Hammond 2023)

uate degree. Although some people were supportive, she again recalled others who tried to dissuade her from continuing her education.

"My first day of class as an undergraduate, I went to the class for premed students," she said. "I was the only girl there, and at the end of the class, the professor comes down and says, 'Young lady, you don't belong here, so you don't need to buy the book. Just go over and talk to the people in the nursing school or in the medical technology school. I'm sure you'll be so much happier if you do that.' I found out what classes were required for medical school, and I never went back to that [Premed Prep] class."

Elizabeth faced countless other hurdles in her academic career.

"I could tell you stories for days about the evils of the way I was treated during medical school," she said.

Elizabeth had a very high MCAT score and perfect grades, but it took persistence for her to be admitted to the University of Utah medical school. While most students with her record were generally admitted after one or two interviews, she had to have a third interview—with the head of the psychiatry department.

"In my interview, he told me that I was taking the place of a man in the class," she said. "He wanted me to recognize that medical school was not something I could just do frivolously because I was smart. I needed to remember that this was a serious obligation. Did I ever intend to get married? Did I ever intend to have children? Did I realize this was a serious job? At that time, I was planning to marry my husband. So, I just put a half-smile on my face, gritted my teeth, and replied to every question. 'Dr. Bliss. I intend to practice medicine my entire life.' I just said that over and over again, and finally, he left me alone—and I got in."

Elizabeth was fortunate to have supportive classmates who stood up for her when the administration made things difficult. She had to have an exploratory laparotomy, diagnostic abdominal surgery in her first year, and the administration attempted to expel her from the school.

"The only reason I didn't get kicked out is that my lab partners went to the dean and said, 'If we take her homework, and we proctor the exam in her room when she's back home from the hospital, will you let her stay?'" she said. The dean agreed, and she was able to continue her classes.

Elizabeth was one of only three women in her class. One quit after her second year because the pressure was so high. Two others transferred from other schools in their third year, and because one was pregnant, the administration tried to kick her out as well.

"She'd been trying to have a baby for nine years," Elizabeth said. "That year I was the president of our class, and so I went to the dean with a petition signed by every student in our class. I said, 'We will do her work. We will make sure that nothing falls through the cracks. But you cannot kick her out.' Ultimately, he agreed to let her stay, but he was very negative about it."

Elizabeth expressed her gratitude for her husband, Jack, and said she didn't know what she would have done without his support to combat the miserable way people treated her.

"To be clear, my classmates, many of whom were male members of the Church, were amazing, supportive, and understanding," she said. "But others—the administration, hospital staff—wouldn't even learn my name. They treated me like it was an amazing accident that I was doing so well in the class. So, I had to be twice as good as everybody else."

Dr. Hammond graduated at the top of her class with high honors and received one of the two awards given to the top graduates. She completed an internship with the University of Utah Health Science Center.

After her internship, she received a fellowship from the National Cancer Institute to study cancer at the Karolinska Institute in Stockholm, Sweden.

"My husband and I spent a year there, which was wonderful, because there was no prejudice against women in science," Elizabeth said.

However, their time in Sweden opened Elizabeth and Jack's eyes to other prejudices, particularly that Black People of The Church of Jesus Christ of Latter-day Saints did not have access to the priesthood or temple blessings.

"We were so frustrated about it that we would spend hours praying about it, fasting about it, and reading things," she said. "We came to the conclusion that it could not be doctrine; it had to be practice."

The couple spoke to the local mission president and their bishop about their concerns, and both men brushed off their questions.

"They asked us if we were paying our tithing, or if we were sleeping with somebody besides each other," Elizabeth recalled. "They implied that we would have to be somebody who's not active if we had these weird concerns about Black people having the priesthood."

Despite the slight, Elizabeth said she and Jack weren't affected or offended by what their leaders had said. They began a pattern of seeking personal revelation for themselves and their family to make sure they were doing what God knew was right for them.

"When I got those kinds of judgmental comments, I would pray about it and talk with my husband. Then we would pray about it together, and we would get the impression that we were OK and that, so far, it was working," she shared. "We didn't see lightning bolts or anything, but we felt that we were being supported in the decisions we were making, and that helped a lot."

After her fellowship in Sweden, Elizabeth and Jack moved to Boston for her residency at Massachusetts General Hospital.

"In Boston, nobody cared that I was a woman as long as I could do the work, so the 1970s, for me, were a wonderful time," she said. "I loved Boston, and I never wanted to go back to Utah."

Elizabeth finished her residency in 1974 and joined the faculty at Harvard Medical School. She was on her way to a tenured position and enjoyed life in Boston, but Jack was miserable in his job as an architect in a large firm that had no room for upward growth. He was offered a full partnership in a firm in Salt Lake City, and while he wanted to take the job and move immediately, Elizabeth was hesitant about returning to Utah.

"I didn't feel much friction when I was living in Boston," she shared. "There wasn't any conflict or criticism in Boston in the LDS circles, because we were all doing our own thing and were mutually supportive."

Elizabeth and Jack decided that she should finish her research award with the Massachusetts Cancer Society and then make the move to Utah. Two years later, they did, and the move proved both difficult and rewarding.

Although they were worried about Church culture in Utah, the couple decided to remain "rock solid" in the faith and attend consistently because they wanted their family to have a habit of participating in the Church.

"I was mindful of the fact that it was going to be a dangerous place for me," Elizabeth said. "I was thinking, 'OK, I have to go back there, but ten years have gone by, so maybe things are better now.'"

They moved to the Avenues neighborhood of Salt Lake City because it was close to Elizabeth's work at LDS Hospital, and they knew it would be a more multicultural environment than some other areas of Utah. However, Elizabeth soon faced some of the same prejudices she had when she'd been a student.

"When I arrived at LDS Hospital, I had a five-month-old baby. People at work were very unhappy that I had a child at home, and I got a lot of awful comments," she said. "That was in the late 1970s when there was a lot of rhetoric in the Church about women staying home and obeying the prophet."

The negative pressure within the Church and the difficulties of balancing her and Jack's work schedules with parenting and family life was challenging. While Elizabeth noted that some couples have terrible stress in their lives if they're both pursuing professional goals and raising their children, she and Jack planned out ways to make it work.

"My biggest blessing in all of this has been my husband. When I would get discouraged, he would say to me, '*We* have too much invested in this for you to give up.'"

Elizabeth said they were both committed to providing and caring for their children, and they balanced their work schedules so that one of them was always able to stay home with the kids.

"If I had to work more, I'd go earlier. If he had to work more, he'd stay later. We had it all figured out," she said.

Elizabeth stated that Jack was her biggest advantage throughout the adversity she faced.

"We were very much in love with each other and committed to our children," she said. "Nobody was going to knock me down, because I had him. If I had a problem, I would just go home and tell him the problem and the two of us would talk it over. He was my psychiatrist, my best friend, and the best dad in the world. I can't say enough good things about him. He was just amazing."

Elizabeth loved being a doctor and a mother in equal parts. She arranged her schedule so that she was able to spend as much time as possible with her kids and raise them with the same love and care she'd had as a child.

"I grew up in a very happy family, and my parents always told me that the greatest joy in life would come from having children. I believed them, and when I had my children, that was where I found all my joy. It was such a wonderful experience to be a parent, and I loved my kids, and I wanted to be with them."

Elizabeth explained that part of the reason she was so successful as both a doctor and a mother was because they allowed her to find a personal balance.

"I knew that both my children and I would be better off if I were working," she said. "I'm a very intense and hard-driving person. Working hard is what I mainly like to do, and if I had tried to stay home with them, I think I might have driven them all nuts."

Beyond providing the opportunity to work, Elizabeth has enjoyed her career in medicine because of its great potential for positive influence in the world.

"One of the reasons why I became a doctor is so I could serve others," she said. "I love serving through medicine."

Despite her assurance that she was doing the right thing for herself and her family, the constant barrage of insults from those in her community weighed on her.

"I had to listen to horrible things said over the pulpit in our ward, especially on Mother's Day," she said. "For a while I wouldn't even go to church on Mother's Day. I refused. I'd stay home and plant flowers and try not to think about what they were saying at church, because it would hurt my feelings so badly. The bishop would say, 'I am so grateful to all the mothers who have followed the prophet and have chosen to stay home with their children.'"

Eventually, these comments took their toll.

"It caused me to walk away from God," Elizabeth admitted. "It hurt my testimony, and for a long time I became bitter and angry. It was destructive to me. I basically stopped calling on God, and my life got a lot more difficult."

Things came to a head when Elizabeth's second son, Tom, returned from his mission. She had three children ranging from age fifteen to twenty-three, was busy at work, was angry at the Church, and felt like God wasn't listening to her. She recalled a day when she was standing on the stairs at home and Tom looked at her and said, "Mom, you just seem so unhappy."

Elizabeth told him he was right. "I went on railing about what the Church leaders were saying, and what was happening to me at work, that I couldn't stand all those things. Then I cried and said, 'I can't say my prayers, Tom. When Dad asks me to say prayers with him, I won't do it. I just feel like there's a black curtain between me and God.'"

Tom asked her to remember a time when she didn't feel that way—a time she felt most strongly that she could hear God. Elizabeth recalled that she first felt truly converted to the Church when she had been dating a young man who wasn't a member of the Church and invited the missionaries to come over to teach him.

"I tried to convert him, and the missionaries converted me instead," she quipped.

Tom told her that since he was a missionary, he could give her the missionary discussions. Elizabeth replied that she already knew the gospel and had lived it all her life, but what Tom said next surprised her.

"He said, 'No, you need to start over, Mom.'"

For the next six weeks, Tom, Elizabeth, and Jack studied the gospel together daily.

"I did exactly what he told me to do," she said. "I read the scriptures he assigned me. I read the Book of Mormon again. I said my prayers. I started reading the scriptures every day. And the black cloud parted, and I saw the sun again."

Elizabeth said her reconnection with God helped her realize that she had created the distance between them.

"I was doing this to myself," she said. "I was choosing to believe that the things that people were saying were critical of me, when that was not the way it was meant."

Elizabeth told me that she realized comments she had interpreted as being inherently critical of her were not always necessarily meant that way, and she decided to change her perspective.

"I was just thinking about it all wrong," she said. "I was not giving them the benefit of the doubt. I was giving them too much power over me. I needed to recommit to the idea that I shouldn't take offense."

Elizabeth decided to forgive the people in her life who had made hurtful comments, and life became a lot easier after that.

"I decided that the only way I was going to be happy was to forgive these people and forget about it. They didn't know what they were doing to me, just like the Savior said: 'Father, forgive them, for they know not what they do.'"

Elizabeth said she felt like a burden had been lifted from her shoulders.

"I could just say, 'I'm not going to take offense by anything now. I feel good about what I'm doing. I feel good about the decisions I'm making. My husband and I have a happy marriage and a strong family, and I'm just going to go forward with my plan.'"

What struck me after hearing Elizabeth's story is that through all the friction she faced from her professional and faith communities, she and Jack continued to work together through discussion and prayer. They learned to recognize how God spoke to them in order to chart their course, and Elizabeth learned how to use the Savior and His teachings to heal herself.

"Friction has its benefits, for sure," she said. "We all know opposition is essential to our progress. We start off with a very simple faith that's based on things we know. But then something comes along and shakes us up and you start to ask yourself, 'What do I really think? What do I really know? What do I really want?'"

Elizabeth compared the experience to falling into a hole, and said we can either get out of it or dwell in it and blame others for pushing us in.

"I wallowed for a while, and then I finally recognized, 'I've got to get out of this hole,'" she said. "You have a crisis, and then as you get out, you get a refined version, a restored version, of what you really believe and care about."

In this way, Elizabeth has used friction to become more like the Savior in her service to others. Elizabeth has discovered that overcoming friction is about giving others the grace and benefit of the doubt, which strengthens our own connection with Christ.

"I've sort of gone back to a sort of simple faith where I want to just focus on what the Savior wants us to do," she told me. "I think if we're here to love each other, we're here to learn from each other, and we can learn when it's miserable. We can learn from the lady in Relief Society who attacks us, or the bishop who says you shouldn't be working outside the home. We can learn from those people if we don't take offense and we allow ourselves to learn. Our testimony and our relationship with God is a personal thing. It has nothing to do with anyone else, and we can either make it flower in the way that is best, or we can make it go away—and I've done both."

How necessary is embracing this approach in our current culture! What if we each expected friction in our lives? What if, when we faced it, we extended grace to those who say things that are legitimately hurtful? Just like having a practicing physician in your Relief Society was a new thing in the 1970s and people weren't sure what to say, given the rhetoric from the Church. We are all going to make blunders that sound like accusations or judgment. Can we look at each other through the Savior's eyes and realize that we truly don't know what we are doing?

The friction we have with others can hamper or promote our relationship with the Divine, depending upon our response. Friction is a sign of movement and progression; there is no resistance if we stand still. In the end, friction is always worth it, because nothing is accomplished without it.

IIIIIIIIIIIIIIIIIIIIIIIIIIIIIIIII

Elizabeth Hammond splits her time between Salt Lake City and San Diego with her husband. She is still involved in the medical community and spends a great deal of time with her children and grandchildren.

"Personal Revelation + the Prophet"

Anabella Castro Vivanco

||||||||||||||||||||||||||||||

Anabella Vivanco's path from a young Guatemalan immigrant of 15 to a source of strength and inspiration in the United States is rooted in faith and perseverance. When she joined the LDS Church at 17, she didn't just find a community; she discovered a place where her joy, laughter, and unshakable belief in God's goodness could truly flourish.

Anabella was born in the bustling heart of Guatemala City, descending from a line of strong, resilient women. Her story is tightly woven with her mother's, who, at just 14, undertook a journey from their remote village to the capital. It was a week-long trek, with their family relying on a single horse. "They only had a horse, and everyone had to walk. There were 10 of them and they would take turns on the one horse, and sleep on the ground. My mother was a fighter. She was a hard worker. She always taught me the right way to live, she always taught me the love of God, and to respect others."

Yet, with some retrospection, Anabella muses on the support the gospel and its community might have offered her mother during her most challenging times. After losing her husband and 3 of her 7 children by the young age of 39, Anabella watched as her mother although maintaining her hard work, descended into depression and drinking as an outlet; which was encouraged by her family and friends. Anabella expressed, "I wish that the Church would have been there to say, 'Come, let me embrace you.'"

Raised Catholic, Annabella's first encounter with the Church was prompted by her mother's desire for her to practice English in Guatemala, which she was not interested in pursuing. Shortly after, her life led her to New York as a nanny at age 15, where she ran into a "Mormon" exhibit at the World's Fair. It wasn't until she was back in Guatemala after her short stint as a nanny that she realized "she wasn't meant to stay in Guatemala" which led to a courageous seven-day bus journey to Los Angeles, a mere $10 to her name, in search of a better life.

Like many people, Anabella came into the LDS church through an invitation to a "party," which was an old school roadshow put on by the Los Angeles stake in the Wilshire building. "I joined the church because it really felt safe. I felt I could go and pray there," Reflecting on that moment, Anabella recalls how her mother's blessing—granted only after confirming that the Church followed Christ—set her on a path that would change her life.

Anabella had a front row seat for the burgeoning growth of the Hispanic congregation within the walls of the Wilshire Blvd LDS building in Los Angeles. Anabella recalls that the Hispanic members wanted to try and integrate with the 'English' ward, but "the bishop of the English ward did not like us and wanted to kick us out of the building." Her perception was that the leadership in the English ward did not want them meeting in the chapel, so they met in the basement and subsequently the annex building. When I asked a few former residents of that "English" ward they said, "Oh our basement was not like a regular basement it was beautiful—and Annex building was gorgeous". The difference between what the English members thought and how the actual members of the Spanish branch perceived the placement of their worship is striking. How many times, without realizing it, do we create friction for other groups by our actions that seem innocent enough from our vantage point? We create friction for others without even realizing it.

Anabella told me that back in the 1960s and early 1970s the members of the Spanish branch used to tell each other that someday the whole building would be full of Hispanic members and instead of being in the basement they would be in the chapel and have grown to take over the whole building. That day is today—in the Wilshire building there is a USC/UCLA ward and the rest of the wards meeting there are largely Hispanic.

Anabella's narrative is not one of succumbing to the friction of integration into a predominantly English-speaking white congregation, but rather, one of embodying the gospel and inviting others to join in its glory.

Anabella's sense of self, and of her standing with God kept her grounded when racial prejudice created friction. "I have a very strong self-esteem. I have never felt that because I'm Hispanic people are going to mistreat me . . . If they have a problem and treat me different because I am Hispanic, I feel it's their ignorance not mine. So, I never felt this church is for only white people, because nobody is better than me. I doesn't matter, I am who I am. And you're going to love me and respect me for who I am the way I am."

After years of service in a geographic ward, a calling to lead the Relief Society of the Spanish Ward would prove to be her crucible. "They called me to be the relief society president and you can hear them gasp . . . You should have seen the faces of those sisters". Anabella articulated that friction that she encountered was because she was not considered one of 'them' after all the years of being in a geographic ward. "They were protecting their own ward, because they wanted a person that was from their own group. But that was very difficult for me. . . . I was there for almost 2 years and every Sunday I would come home crying."

A couple of weeks after being in that calling a sister asked to speak to her. "She said, 'I don't like you. You are so arrogant; you think you are better than us.' Then after she had said all the nasty things to me. I grabbed her hand, and I said, 'Sister, I want you to know this is not my choice. I'm here because they called me. The Lord called me. And I want you to know how much love he has for you, and I would love to have that same love for you.'"

When tensions began to stir within the very walls where she served, her response was rooted in deep faith and humility. Instead of letting mistrust harden her heart, she chose to reach out with kindness, embodying the love and acceptance she sought to foster. Anabella reflects, "I had to stay because I knew that, as they say, my blessings would be greater—and now, whenever there's a ward gathering, we're always invited."

Anabella's life has been a mosaic of varied roles—cosmetologist, esthetician, electrologist, and tireless worker—all harmonized by her devotion to her family and faith. Her journey from Guatemala to the arms factories of Los Angeles marked her pursuit of a better life. "I can work and make a better life; I have always been trying to better myself. I never stopped trying to better myself. I am 76 and I still work," she states, her work ethic undimmed by time.

Marriage at 18 in 1967 and motherhood soon after, didn't quell her aspirations of betterment. When she was first married, her husband, who was a recent émigré from Chile and LDS convert, wisely suggested that she would need to have a career in case anything happened to him. Styling hair had always been something Anabella had a gift for. "My husband paid for a course in cosmetology, he hired a nanny for our 6-month-old. We didn't have the money, but he paid for the nanny so I could go to school. . . . I got my license in 9 months then I went to work in Beverly Hills. I was doing so good because I was learning and making really good money. And then my husband said, 'Ok, you have shown everybody that you can make money.' So, I quit, but people started asking me if could do it at my house. So, I started doing it at my home. Then another woman needed help cleaning her house, and I started doing that for extra money."

Anabella combined her professional pursuit and maternal dedication, by obtaining additional schooling and juggling her career to be available for her children. "I got a job during the hours when my children were in school. I was always there for my children's games, plays, and volunteer opportunities."

To this day, Anabella continues to work at least 2 days a week. When asked, she says, "I work for me. It's for me. I need to have something for me, and I deserve it. You know we all need a therapist. And when I go to work, I'm their therapist and they are mine". It's clear Anabella loves people and considers it a joy to mingle with people, to learn from them and to share her light with them. She also sees the need to demonstrate more than one dimension as a woman, so that your children have a model to follow. "I worked, but I also volunteered, I was always volunteering. We can also be mothers and we can teach our children to be the best, not only for ourselves, but for the world."

When asked about the 1970s and the movement around women's rights, juxtaposed with some of the messaging inside the LDS Church, Anabella had a characteristic response. "It didn't affect me in a way because I had left my country, I had the freedom to come to this country and I felt that it was my blessing, my opportunity to become who I am." She also had a healthy view of the tension within the church around women's issues and found solace in her standing with her Heavenly Father. "I feel that I have the right to say what I believe and what I want to my husband. Because he respects me, and I respect him. I also have the freedom to choose. He has never stopped me from choosing anything that I want to do. Sometimes we disagree on certain things, but he never pushes me, He lets me find out by myself if I am right or wrong. I have the Priesthood; Women have the Priesthood and I've been able to use it. It doesn't mean that I have to go in front of people and put my hands on somebody's head to bless them. But I have the right to have the Priesthood because I am a daughter of God."

Friction was a friend to Anabella because of her deep belief in the gospel of Jesus Christ. "There were always women that didn't agree with what I was doing. They believe different than you. But you just have to ignore them, or 'this is what you believe, and I respect you, but I want you to respect what I believe'. I never had any problems with anyone arguing or anything like that because I always said 'that's good that you believe that, but I don't believe in that and don't try to change my feelings'. . . . I am a very strong person and I have always felt the Lord protecting me and guiding me. I can be one of his warriors, I mean, I am not perfect, but if I wanted to do something I would do it as long as it is something that is going to help me get to be a better person. Not to try to please other people, because that route can destroy you. . . . Why are you going to change somebody's ideas? Why are we going to change somebody's way of doing things when we don't want them to change us?"

Her advice was to listen to both your own personal revelation and the prophet to be able to navigate any friction or question you have. "The prophet is the Lord sending me a message that I need to have, but I need personal revelation for my family, my work or anything. I have to listen to both."

In her 76 years she has seen how the gospel has blessed her life and family's. "I have always known what the gospel teaches me and where I stand in here [heart] because I can see the hands of the Lord working on me and in my family."

Her journey is one illuminated by personal revelation, guided by the wisdom of the prophet, and enriched by the gospel. At 76, Anabella's life is a testament to the transformative power of faith, a beacon for others navigating their own paths. Her message to younger women resonates with the clarity of experience: "It's difficult because the world has changed, what used to be good is bad. And what used to be bad is good. So, you have to be architects of your own destiny. Because whatever decision you are going to be making in life is going to affect you now, in the near future or in the long run."

||||||||||||||||||||||||||||||||

Anabella Vivanco lives in Southern California, spends time each day engaging with People. Her two daughters and one son have brought joy into her life along with grandchildren that Anabella dotes on.

"I Know That I Know"

Anne Osborn Poelman

|||||||||||||||||||||||||||||||

A world-renowned authority on neuroradiology[1], Anne Osborn Poelman is a study in contrasts. She's brilliant and has an extraordinary résumé, but she's down to earth and humble. Like most academics, she questions and challenges long-held beliefs, yet she joined the Church in the middle of medical school after two naive young missionaries gave her the discussions using a flannel board. She's literally written the textbook on diagnostic imaging of the brain, but she's also the author of religious books for an LDS audience. She was the first female president of the American Neuroradiology Society and also served on the Sunday School General Board and Relief Society General Board. Some things concern her about the Church, but she has a rock-solid testimony of the gospel.

---

1. A subspeciality of diagnostic radiology that focuses on diagnosing abnormalities in the central or peripheral nervous system.

But none of these seeming incongruities feel discordant to Anne. There's no dissonance in her life; all her seemingly opposing facets are actually complementary and make up who she is. She's exceptionally self-aware and has her eyes wide open, especially when it comes to friction between Church teachings and her personal beliefs, about what's right for her.

"It's not that we don't see issues in the Church and don't say, 'You know, that troubles me,'" Anne said in an interview with me at her home in Salt Lake City. "Some things trouble me a great deal. But because of that, can we be honest enough with ourselves and say, 'I'm here because I need to be here'?"[2]

Anne is no stranger to personal revelation. After graduating from Stanford with a major in psychology, she went to Harvard to pursue a PhD. But one day, she had an experience that changed the course of her life.

"I was on the way from the MTA train stop to the Mass General hospital and it struck me that I needed to go to medical school. I understood in that moment that it was true, and I almost got run over because I stopped in the middle of the street. I realized that I was in the wrong place doing the wrong thing; that what I needed to do was to go into medicine, and to go back to Stanford. I knew that just as surely as I was standing there."

Anne called her professor at Stanford and told him about her epiphany. Applications for med school were already past due, but the professor was on the admissions committee and said he'd talk to the other members. She was accepted, even though she hadn't taken all the required pre-med courses as

---

2. (Poelman 2023)

an undergrad. (She finished all of them prior to starting school that fall.)

Among all the superb professors at the Stanford School of Medicine, one stood out. She learned that he was a member of The Church of Jesus Christ of Latter-day Saints, a religion she didn't know much about.

"Here was this professor we all admired," Anne remembered. "He used to win the Teacher of the Year Award from the medical students, not only because he was a great teacher, but because he really cared about the students."

The professor's character and demeanor piqued Anne's interest in the Church. An LDS family she knew invited the missionaries to give her the lessons in their home, but when they showed up, they were not at all what she was expecting.

"When the family told me they were going to invite 'the elders,' they didn't tell me that the elders were younger than I was," Anne said. "I'm not making this up—it was the junior companion's turn to give his first discussion of his mission. He reached into his briefcase and pulled out a flannel board! He put this thing up, and he started to tell me the plan of salvation, the plan of happiness. I was sitting there totally dumbfounded."

Anne was a dazzling student at one of the best medical schools in the world, and here was an earnest fresh-faced missionary sticking a round object on a flannel board and saying, "Sister Osborn, this is the Earth."

"I suppose if my jaw had been untethered, it would have been hanging down around my ankles," Anne told me with a laugh. The elder "pulled out this kind of sunlight thing" and told her it was the celestial kingdom. "Then he forgot what the next thing was because he was a greenie, and then he just looked me in the eye and said, 'Sister Osborn, I know the gospel's true.' With this naive, incredible, but very meaningful belief."

She was baptized in 1968, in the middle of med school. Her academic advisor, when he heard the news, thought Anne had lost her mind and called her into his office.

"He wanted to know if I was OK," Anne recalled. "He said, 'Have you joined the Mormon Church because your boyfriend jilted you or something like that? Is that why you've done something crazy?'" This was the San Francisco Bay Area during the Flower Power era—not the most hospitable place for a religion, especially one that apparently discriminated against Black People and women.

Anne was unfazed by the criticism nor was she swayed by new information that unfolded about the Church.

"I was at a dinner party maybe five months after I had converted, and they explained to me what 'the garment' was," she told me during our interview. "It was very unsettling, not for what it represented but because it made me wonder, *If they haven't told me about this, what other things don't I know?* It turns out there were a lot. But by the time some of those came along, I had the context in which to put things in and the testimony in which to put things on. I've never, ever doubted. I've been able to make the distinction between the gospel and the Church. Some people don't think there is a distinction, but there is."

After graduating from Stanford, Anne accepted a surgery internship in Salt Lake City at LDS Hospital, a hospital that had never had a female intern or resident before. Her attending physician was a trailblazer in cardiothoracic surgery: Russell M. Nelson.[3]

"To me, he was this near deity-like figure because of his reputation as a surgeon," Anne said. "He taught me a lot and was unbelievably supportive and respectful. I felt extraordinarily fortunate to be his intern."

After returning to Stanford for her residency, she decided to accept an offer to join the faculty of the University of Utah School of Medicine. In eight years, Anne went from instructor to full professor—an extremely fast trajectory, especially since the U had never had a tenure-track woman in radiology before. Not too long after that, she began lecturing around the world. Today, at age eighty, she's working on the third edition of *Osborn's Brain*, the authoritative textbook on brain imaging for neuroradiologists, neurosurgeons, and neurologists.

"It's been a great blessing to me to have had my professional life," Anne said, "and to have that part of me removed from the Church part. But was it easy? No. The easiest part was the part that I had inside, the feeling that when I heard the gospel and began to understand what it really was—not the flannel board version. It sounded familiar; like somehow, someplace, I had heard and seen those things before."

That feeling was what kept Anne solidly in the Church, even when it was sometimes uncomfortable being around other LDS women who were not professionals—women who were staying home with their children because the prophet had told them to.

---

3. Russell M Nelson was called as an Apostle of The Church of Jesus Christ of Latter-Day Saints in 1984, and was set apart as the 17th President of the Church of Jesus Christ of Latter-Day Saints January 14, 2018

"On the occasions when I went to Relief Society," she recalled, "I would sit in the back of the room and read my scriptures and try to block out what was being said. I guess, if I paid attention, it would have been hurtful. I knew a lot of the women and I liked them, and I knew that they liked me. But they were in an organization. Although I felt accepted personally, when you're listening to a 'cultural refinement' lesson, and hearing this and that, it just seemed irrelevant for me."

A time came when Anne had to make a choice: Should she stop going to Relief Society? She asked herself, *Why do you need other people?*

"Some say, 'I don't need an organization,'" Anne said. "They say 'I can go hiking or do yoga, take a walk in the foothills with the two golden retrievers, and I will feel a lot more spiritual than I will if I'm sitting in the chapel on 18th Avenue with someone droning on and on a talk where they forget to mention the Savior.' Does that happen? Of course it does. But then there are far more times when you leave a Church meeting and say, 'You know, it was really wonderful.'"

She answered her own question—*Why do you need other people?*—with this thoughtful response:

"Here in this ward, everybody has a story. Everybody has a history, everybody has issues, and nobody cares. And that's what is really important. So, yes, I know that I know. What keeps me in is that I also know that I need it. Am I strong enough to depend solely on myself? No. That would be really spiritually arrogant to say, 'I don't need that. I can study the scriptures on my own.' We all need each other. Nobody is strong enough to do this by himself or herself. So, the Church as an organization, as flawed as it is, is also as great as it is."

Anne expressed the hope that "we're all in the Church because of Christ and the opportunity to serve each other. That's why I go. If you look for reasons to toss it all out, you can find plenty, because it's an organization of fallible human beings."

Noting the difference between Church culture and the gospel, Anne said that "practices change and the culture changes, and attitudes shift over time. We've seen that happen. Things evolve. Are there things that I wish were different? Absolutely. There always will be.But I know that I know the basic core principles of the gospel, and I think it's my gift. I think you have to focus on the fundamentals: your testimony of the Savior; your belief in the core principles of the gospel; that the Savior is who He says He is and did what He did; that the basic principles of the gospel are eternal; that the principles and foundation of the gospel are unchanging. Everything else is noise."

As I listened to Anne, I kept thinking about four words she said: "Was it easy? No." Why are we surprised when we encounter friction at church? One of our core beliefs is that there is opposition "in all things," so why wouldn't there be opposition at Church? Why do would staying in the Church should be easy? I left our conversation thinking there will always be friction in an organization—it's what we do with that resistance that makes the difference.

Another five words struck me as simple but very complex and critical: "I know that I know." We often forget that inspiration comes to all God's children, because He cares about each of us individually. He teaches us how to recognize that inspiration and to have confidence to know He was involved in each of our unique paths.

I asked Anne about that moment walking from the train stop when she had the sudden thought to become a doctor. Did she recognize that that thought was inspiration for her unique path? She responded that there had been a few critical times in her life when "she knew that she knew" and realized that feeling of certainty and conviction was from God. And that is what has driven Anne Osborn Poelman in her life: knowing she knew.

Community

Judith Rasmussen Dushku

|||||||||||||||||||||||||||||||||

Judy Dushku's experiences with friction in the Church have been numerous, but they have taught her to show compassion to those who see things differently. As a professor, writer, and activist, she has dedicated her life to using education and understanding to foster positive growth, and she has plowed ahead past any conflict she's encountered.

Judy graduated from BYU in 1964 with a degree in political science. After her graduation, she decided to apply to the Fletcher School, a prestigious graduate school for international studies at Tufts University. She asked one of her professors for a letter of recommendation, but he was reluctant.

"He wrote me a letter, but he said, 'Honestly, Judy, you'd do better if you just went to Washington. I could help you find a job being an executive assistant to one of the congresspeople for Utah. That's the way women get power in Washington, D.C.,'" she recalled him saying. "That was the approach. Nobody encouraged me. Nobody cheered me on when I got accepted and got a scholarship."[1]

At Fletcher, Judy was one of two members of the Church in her PhD program. She described the environment as an entirely new culture, and recalled how she and the other student were given their own nonalcoholic punch bowl at events.

"They kind of enjoyed it," she said. "They'd say, 'This is for the Mormon students.'"

She did well in the program, but she didn't love it. She intended to stick it out and finish her PhD anyway, but a former boyfriend told her about a job opportunity as an assistant professor of political science at Suffolk University in Boston.

She took the job, and there she found her calling. She had originally deferred her PhD program at Fletcher and only planned on taking a year off, but she told the school to terminate her participation in the program. They had a secondary master's degree, called a Masters in Law and Diplomacy, and she received that instead.

For forty-seven years, Judy taught a wide range of classes at Suffolk.

"My best courses, and most popular ones, were women and public policy, African politics, and Soviet and post-Soviet politics," she said. "I loved it. And I was a really good teacher, and I kept getting Professor of the Year and all that. So, it was just fun to be there. I felt appreciated."

Judy first started teaching in the late 1960s, when there was considerable unrest around civil rights, the Vietnam War, and

---

1. (Dushku 2023)

women's rights. Judy was part of a consciousness-raising group at her university that helped her understand and address those issues, and she soon joined a second: the group of Latter-day Saint women in Boston that included Laurel Thatcher Ulrich, Jill Mulvay Derr, Claudia Bushman, Christine Durham, Elizabeth Hammond, Grethe Peterson, and others.

"I also had this Mormon group that I just loved," Judy said. "We started meeting in the 1960s, but not really around anything specific. I went to all the gatherings that we had for our group."

The women took turns meeting at the church building or each other's houses. Judy recalled a rule she suggested early on in the forming of the group: Whoever was hosting had to commit to not clean their bathroom before the meeting.

"It takes so much time, and so much useless energy is spent," Judy explained. "We were going to meet in the mornings, when their kids were in school. We had to promise—*I will not clean the bathroom.* I remember loving going to different people's bathrooms."

This helped set a tone for the meetings. They were places without judgment or prerequisites, and they allowed these women to work out social issues from a gospel perspective.

"Honestly, the Mormon women's group was as eager and as well read and as open to discussion as any group in the city of Boston," Judy said. "But anyway, it was a radical group, and a completely safe group . . . They were really great. We would literally give assignments to the group: Let's do this, let's read this, let's watch that video."

Judy was kept busy attending the consciousness-raising group and working full-time. She also got married in 1969 and had four children by 1980, so she had a lot to balance, but the work didn't stop there. The women's group was inspired by learning about previous generations of LDS women that actively created spaces for dialogue through the *Woman's Exponent* (1872–1914). The group started teaching Institute classes, made a "pink issue" of *Dialogue*, and started their own newspaper.

Judy recalled Susan Kohler finding the copies of the *Woman's Exponent* in the Harvard library, and told me they had originally tried to get something about it published in a Church magazine. Judy wrote a letter to the *Ensign*, explaining what they had found and asking if they could publish something about it in the magazine.

"I got a call from a woman at the *Ensign*," Judy said. "She said, 'You're crazy if you think we're going to put this in the *Ensign*. They have to be more subtle, and your article is just too upfront.'"

Judy told me the group didn't want to keep their findings to themselves; they saw it as a veritable treasure trove. They wrote letters to General Authorities, trying to see if anyone in the Church would be interested in sharing more about the *Woman's Exponent*, but the group never heard back. This didn't deter any of the women; in fact, it only made them more resourceful. They collaborated on their issue of *Dialogue*, called the "pink issue" because it focused on Latter-day Saint women and because the front cover was literally pink.

"It was not intended to be pink," Judy told me. "The printer had printed it on pink paper . . . because the printer was out of white regular paper. Such a lazy thing to do, but we literally just owned it—like, this is a pink issue of *Dialogue.*"

The pink issue helped get the word out about their group, and people were interested in learning more about women in the history of the Church.

"A really lovely man who was the director of the LDS Institute at Cambridge said, 'You guys, why don't you teach an Institute class? You've been doing all this research. No one's listening, right? You do an Institute class, and every week, a different one of you will present,'" Judy recalled. "So that's why we wrote these pieces."

Those Institute classes formed the foundation for *Mormon Sisters: Women in Early Utah*, which the group later published. They also continued sharing their stories in the newspaper they started, the *Exponent II.* There was some negative feedback, as discussed in the upcoming chapter about Claudia Bushman, but the response was largely positive.

"We were discouraged that we had so little support, but it didn't feel like the whole Church was against us because he was our Institute director, inviting us," Judy said. "And lots of people came, but nobody treated us like we were really odd. I honestly didn't believe that the Church was against the *Exponent II* and all that. I thought it was this wonderful thing and that it was our job to teach the Church."

Being a part of a community and being able to use her talents limited friction for Judy. She was able to bounce ideas off others and learn from diverse points of view. Her group ruffled a lot of feathers, but she found that this chafing allowed her to deepen her understanding of the issues she addressed.

Judy had plenty of additional experiences that cemented the importance of loving and appreciating those with viewpoints different from her own. One stands out to her because it taught her an additional lesson about sisterhood within the Church.

Judy had gone as a representative from her stake to a White House conference on families in the mid '70s in Washington, D.C. She was pregnant at the time and was vomiting from the nausea, and while she had planned on taking an eight-hour train back home, another LDS sister from central Massachusetts offered to drive her home. Judy found on her drive that they had very different ideologies.

"So, she drove me home and we tried to talk about the conference, but she was so appalled by everything that I believed and was doing," Judy said. "I knew at the time I got to Boston, after eight hours of vomiting, that she was not an ally. And then she showed up at different stake things over the next year and she said all the wrong things, but I felt so grateful, because she drove me when I was pregnant and sick. It was one of these things where my "sisterhoodly" feeling about Relief Society overruled my hostility toward everything she stood for."

This sister had very different ideological beliefs from Judy, but she had showed her incredible charity, and they were united by their faith in Christ and their membership in the Church. Judy pointed out that when someone doesn't agree with your ideology, it doesn't mean you should discount them, but love them. This was true even of her relationship with Church leadership, despite the conflict her group's writing had caused with them. When I asked Judy if she ever thought of not participating in the Church, her answer was definitive.

"No one talked about leaving the Church back then. When we got angry, no one ever said, 'I'm walking out.' That's a 2010 issue."

Judy told me she has felt anger at times, but she has learned to temper it and speak in ways that promote understanding and peace.

"Just choose your remarks carefully," she said. "I'm really good at being non-angry, but I can be angry too. I'm such a Mormon that I've learned how to speak Relief Society."

I asked Judy what she would say to the rising generation, particularly those facing friction within the organization of the Church.

"You think people are on the opposite side from you, when they're actually not," she advised me. "I think people will agree with us more than we expect. And I'd say speak up, speak up, speak up. Once you speak up, you'll have all these new friends who will say, 'Oh, you're just like me!' And then you'll find out that you are alike."

Judy is a delightful, amazing person. Since retiring from Suffolk, she has written numerous articles and even won first place in the "Mormon Women Speak" contest. She now spends her time writing and managing a nonprofit that works in Uganda to alleviate some of the suffering women experience. She continues to contemplate how to affect the lives of women, not only in the United States but also around the world. She sees the value in community, and when friction comes, as it has in all kinds of ways for her, she has learned to lean on her community to work things out and love those around her.

Something to Think About

Claudia Lauper Bushman

⁙⁙⁙⁙⁙⁙⁙⁙⁙⁙⁙⁙⁙⁙⁙⁙⁙⁙⁙⁙⁙⁙⁙⁙⁙⁙⁙

For Claudia Lauper Bushman, the friction she has felt as she's balanced life as a mother, academic, and Latter-day Saint has never caused her to question her faith. On the contrary—it has helped her grow.

"My question is not why I stay in the Church, but why should I leave?" she once wrote. "I love the Church. Why would I even think of leaving it? I'm happy here. I certainly hope and pray that the Church does not decide to leave me."[1]

Claudia's life has been marked by constant progress and action. She is a distinguished American historian and a notable figure in the study of American religious history. Throughout her prolific career, she has made significant contributions to the field, particularly in the exploration of the history of The

---

1. (Rees 2011)

Church of Jesus Christ of Latter-day Saints and the experiences of women within the context of religion.

Claudia's deep understanding of American religious history is showcased in her influential works, including *Mormon Sisters: Women in Early Utah* (1976) and *Building the Kingdom: A History of Mormons in America* (2001). In these groundbreaking books, she examines the roles and contributions of women within the early Mormon community and provides a comprehensive account of the growth and evolution of the LDS Church in American society. She also founded the Mormon Women Oral History Project at Claremont Graduate University and was founding editor of the Exponent II.

In addition to her scholarly endeavors, Claudia has been a dedicated mentor and educator. She served as a professor of American studies and religious studies at Columbia University, where she inspired countless students to pursue rigorous academic inquiry and engage critically with history and religion.

As an active member of the Church, Claudia has been deeply involved in its community and has worked to promote dialogue and understanding. Her involvement in the Relief Society organization has allowed her to explore the intersection of gender, faith, and community. She has also been an advocate for women's voices within the Church, working to highlight their contributions and foster inclusivity.

"I certainly admit that women are not equally treated in the Church," she told me. But instead of growing angry or disillusioned, Claudia has maintained her independence and desire for action. She shared a sentiment she's commonly quoted for:

"Why don't you just make a list of all the things you would do if you had the priesthood? And make that list and then just do those things anyway—which you can do. I do all the things I want."

Claudia first encountered friction both within the Church and American society when she got married her junior year of college at Wellesley.

"When I married Richard, I picked off the best man around and became a student wife," she said. "Because I was still in college, I definitely lost caste. Being a wife just canceled out being a student. Being a wife doesn't have a lot of status."

Claudia enjoyed marriage and looked forward to starting a family, and she planned on being done with school after she finished at Wellesley.

"If I could just get that degree, then I would just quit," she recalled. "But I hadn't been out of school for any time at all until I was hungry to get back."

She signed up for three classes at the Lowell Institute, an education foundation in Boston.

"I just didn't feel I had anything to think about without school," she said. "I had to have something to think about. So, from then on, I tried to always do something like that."

She certainly did. While she didn't originally plan to get a doctorate, she spent about a decade in graduate school, completing her master's at BYU and her PhD at Boston University. She experienced friction as she pursued her advanced degrees because she was following a different path. She stuck out.

"I certainly felt that I was different from other people," she shared. "I was a graduate student. I had five children, then I had my sixth—and nobody else was even married. And I know there were people who thought I had no business being in graduate school at all, but I just wanted to do it. Plenty of people thought I was an odd bird, doing these crazy things that I did."

Claudia said she didn't particularly desire a career, as she had plenty of fulfilling work at home with her family, but always sought after mentally stimulating enrichment.

"I wasn't one who was yearning to get away from home. I just needed something else," she explained. "I had to have things to do."

Throughout her life, having things to do and things to think about drove Claudia to continually keep moving regardless of any friction she felt. She prized the forward movement of growth and pushed through any conflict.

In her essay in *Why I Stay: The Challenges of Discipleship for Contemporary Mormons*, Claudia wrote, "Of course I have had some pretty horrific experiences that would have persuaded many to leave. I could give a very salty talk about putdowns I have experienced and insults I have borne."

Claudia turned to action and community to ease the pain of those wounds and make the Church community a more welcoming one. We have seen that a common thread in dealing with friction is to find a community to learn with and discuss questions and concerns through a gospel lens. However, Claudia explained that just discussing isn't enough; one must take action as well. She focused on projects that created a way for her to use her talents in her community and create more learning opportunities for others.

Claudia was part of the group of Latter-day Saint women based in Boston in the 1970s that formed such a community. They would gather to discuss women's issues and work on different projects. One of the first began as a small undertaking to present to students at the Church's local institutes of religion program but developed into an entire book.

"We did a class where we each took a topic and did research and presented those to the institute. We decided, well, we're going to write them up. We did *Mormon Sisters* out of that."

Mormon Sisters: Women in Early Utah was considered groundbreaking at the time it was published. Claudia and her collaborators started and funded their own printing press in order to publish it—although there was such demand for it twenty years later, in 1997, that Utah State University reprinted it.

Claudia recalled other projects the group had worked on, such as a yearly Exponent Day Dinner that they hosted in honor of the Woman's Exponent. They would charge for the dinner and fly out interesting guest speaks that allowed women in the community to come together and learn from different guests.

"The [one of] the first years, I think, we had Juanita Brooks, which was really something, and she was thrilled to come," she said. "She stayed with us and brought me several of her books, and she spoke to this large group that came to dinner."

Perhaps the group's greatest achievement was the founding of *Exponent II*, a quarterly periodical focused on Latter-day Saint women's stories.

"One time I came home from an event that we'd done, and I said, 'Well, everything we do just turns to gold. What should we do next?'" Claudia recalled. "And Richard said, 'Start a newspaper.'"

Despite being busy with graduate school and editing *Mormon Sisters*, Claudia worked with her friends to get started and became the editor of *Exponent II*.

It was difficult to get running at first. Some women wanted to be involved but simply didn't have the time on top of their family responsibilities and Church callings, and those who were able to contribute had to squeeze in the time and cobble together resources.

"At the beginning, Susan Koehler, who was married to a chemistry professor, typed out the whole issue on her husband's typewriter after hours," Claudia said. "And then because she made lots of mistakes, she would have to start each line over again."

They started publishing *Exponent II* and soon received positive responses. Judy Dushku, one of the founders of the periodical, mentioned that they had four thousand subscribers to start.

"People were very taken with it," Claudia said. "It was a great experience for all of us. And it's still going. Pretty impressive, don't you think? After all these years."

It's been over fifty years since the genesis of *Exponent II*, but as I listened to Claudia, I could tell those years have not diminished either her energy or her sense of accomplishment.

"It was great, gave us all a good life," she said. "We would work together and do something that nobody could do, and . . . it gave us an important project to do. That's for me what the empowering thing is: to do something."

Empowering to do something. When we run up against friction, it's an easy option to just stop. However, Claudia focused on doing something to use that friction to grow, and that's what has helped keep her testimony strong all these years. I also love how she said that her projects gave her and her collaborators a life. That's the benchmark: having something to do that enriches you and also benefits your community.

While the *Exponent II* received a lot of support, it was met with mixed reactions. Many people, including a large contingent of women, were hungry for the essays, viewpoints, and thought pieces that opened and sometimes challenged their worldview. However, because of the conflict surrounding women's roles in the Church at that time, some who weren't so happy that a group of so-called 'housewives from Boston' were publishing an unofficial LDS women's viewpoint paper. Claudia was eventually asked by a General Authority to step down from being the editor of the *Exponent II, with the explanation that it conflicted with her husband standing as the Stake President of the Boston Stake at the time,* which Claudia has called one of the most painful moments of her life. It created a lot of friction, and Claudia had to balance her family, her church, and her passion. She chose to step down from being editor, but she continued her exploration as a historian of the LDS Church. She continued to cultivate the friendships she had forged to lessen the tension in her life.

The cost of participation was high for Claudia, but she told me that the benefits, in her eyes, were worth it. Multiple times during our interview, Claudia talked about never really thinking about leaving the Church, even in her most painful moments.

"I never have felt that everybody has to believe the way I believe. I never get up and say things like, 'I know that this is the true way,'" she told me. "But I'm a lifer. I'm going to stick around."

Claudia pointed specifically to the sense of community and opportunities to develop her talents within the Church as some of the things that bring her the most joy.

"I get plenty of things to do in the Church, and I love them. It's been a great opportunity for me to use whatever skills I've got," she said.

On multiple occasions, Claudia has said, "Everything I ever needed to know, I learned at church, and I still call on the lessons I learned there every day." She reiterated that sentiment quite a few times to me during our interview. She talked about presenting, musicals, learning, and more as skills she has learned in the Church, but I kept thinking that the thing she learned how to do most was to use the friction she encountered to spur her on to more learning, more growth, more of everything.

Claudia Lauper Bushman's contributions as a historian, advocate, and member of the LDS Church have left an indelible mark on the field of American religious history. Her insightful research, passionate advocacy, and commitment to promoting dialogue and inclusivity have enriched our understanding of the Church and the experiences of women within religious communities. Claudia's enduring legacy serves as an inspiration to scholars, religious practitioners, and individuals seeking a more nuanced understanding of American religious life.

"We Have to
Educate Each Other"

Melba Kooyman

IIIIIIIIIIIIIIIIIIIIIIIIIIIIII

Growing up as a young woman in the 1950s, Melba Kooyman felt she had three career options: nursing, teaching, or secretarial work. But after receiving her Registered Nursing license and working as an RN she wanted to continue her education. She received a master's degree and worked as a professor of nursing education for over twenty years, teaching and inspiring thousands of students at a time when few women taught at the collegiate level and few Latter-day Saint women worked outside the home.

Melba's love for education has been a motivator throughout her life that has encouraged her to decipher the paradoxes and uncertainties she encountered, both in her career and in her faith. The friction she has faced has become a tool wielded as leverage to keep learning and growing.

Born in Ogden, Utah, but a current resident of Del Mar, California, Melba has spent most of her life living in those two states. Her parents weren't active in the Church, but her grandparents and many of her friends were, so she often attended Church activities with them. Melba's parents were divorced, and her mother had to work long hours to provide for herself and the family, including the grandparents. So, Melba spent a lot of time with her grandmother.

"My grandmother, Lillian Thomas Agee, and I did everything together," Melba told me. "We enjoyed attending church and getting acquainted with local members. . . . She was my nourisher."[1]

Her grandmother would often bear her testimony to Melba and encouraged her to build a foundation of faith that would sustain her throughout her life.

"Now, don't you listen to your aunts and uncles, because they they've had a falling out with the Church," her grandmother would say. "The gospel is true. Joseph Smith was a prophet of God. I really know that to be true, and I want you to believe that."

Her grandmother taught her to study the gospel and continually seek out learning, and this encouraged Melba in various aspects of her life. When she graduated high school in 1954, she wanted to continue her education. One of her aunts was a nurse, and Melba was inspired to follow her path.

"My family always said, 'Be a nurse, you can always get a job,'" Melba recalled. "And that was sort of the mantra from the family because they all suffered during the Depression years.

---

1. (Kooyman 2023)

Getting an education was the ticket to getting a job, so that was high on my list."

Melba attended San Jose Hospital School of Nursing at San Jose State to get her nursing license before transferring to the University of Utah in 1957 to finish her bachelor's degree. After graduating in 1959, she started working at the County Hospital in Salt Lake City, but the work was disappointing; she wanted something else. At the time, United Airlines was hiring flight attendants with nursing licenses for overwater flights, so Melba signed up. She worked as a flight attendant in San Francisco from 1960 to 1962, working on countless long flights from San Francisco to Hawaii, as well as other domestic destinations.

While living in San Francisco, Melba continued her spiritual education. When she attended nursing school in San Jose, she spent time in the local Latter-day Saint Institute of Religion program. It was an amazing religious experience for her and grounded her in the gospel in a way she hadn't been during her childhood, when her church attendance was more sporadic. She continued attending Institute classes at the University of Utah with Lowell Bennion, a well-known Latter-day Saint educator, which was also enriching. However, Melba's time at the LDS Berkeley Institute while she lived in San Francisco was the most memorable because it cemented for her how to blend the gospel with intellectual pursuits.

"The Berkeley LDS Institute would make your testimony soar," Melba said. "Everyone was so supportive of gospel living, but in a way that encompassed your intellectual strivings."

The Berkeley Institute was important for another reason: it was where Melba met her husband, Jerry, who was a graduate student at UC Berkeley at the time.

They married in 1962, and the experience was yet another strengthening spiritual experience. Despite having no family with them, they felt loved and supported when they were sealed.

"We got married that summer in the Logan Temple," Melba told me. "And we had no active family members to accompany us; we went there by ourselves. The temple workers said to us, 'Where are your witnesses?' And we said, 'Well, we are just here on our own; we thought there would be someone here that we could use.' And the wedding party ahead of us had tons of people, and so they gave us some of their witnesses.

"When I got to the dressing room, the woman helping me said, 'I have the perfect dress for you. Many brides donate their dresses afterwards to the temple, just for situations like this. So, we have a closet full of wedding dresses, and I have one that will fit you perfectly.' And so, she put me in this dress. I'm telling you; it was gorgeous. It takes your breath away. Beautiful long sleeves, lace buttons all down the back. It was a really beautiful dress, and Jerry was so surprised."

Melba said those coincidences showed her both God's involvement in her life and the benefit of the Church structure.

"That's just another memory that logs in my mind about the generosity of the Saints," she said. "We want to celebrate people, honor them, when they're making good choices in their lives. And so that was another little chunk of the testimony of the Church that will always be with me."

Shortly after getting married, Jerry started a program at the University of Arizona in Tucson, and Melba started as an assistant professor of nursing at the same university. It was a wonderful experience and her students loved her, but the dean told her she had to get a master's degree if she wanted to continue teaching in a university nursing program.

Melba was excited to continue her education and decided to attend graduate school back in San Francisco at UCSF.

"In the 1960s, UCSF was the 'Who's Who' in medicine, the best speakers, the best classes," Melba said. "I lived in the dorm to save money. It was one of the best years of my life, I have to tell you, because everyone just couldn't wait to get up and go to class. We couldn't wait to go to the library. It was just fabulous."

Melba worked on her degree while Jerry did research in Antarctica; he was the first scientific investigator to design and construct a Time Depth Recorder (TDR) that could measure diving depths and submergence time for marine mammals. She received her master's in 1964.

Melba then continued to teach at the University of Arizona until Jerry's career moved them to San Diego. They had two children by then, and she continued to work part-time as a professor of nursing at Palomar College. Once her children were a bit older, she continued teaching full-time, and did so until 1998. Melba said she continued her career not because of the income, but because she loved learning about health and being engaged in the education process.

"It was gratifying," she shared. "It was really a great experience. And I'm bragging, but I did win the Distinguished Faculty Award while I was teaching there, the highest honor you can get at the college. I love teaching and I really like to help people learn. It wasn't just a job for me. It was really an engagement."

Melba applied this same desire to learn to her relationship with the Church. Talking to her, you get the sense that she has seen it all and somehow was able to roll with the punches. One of the first things that she mentioned being challenging in the Church was the policy around Black People and the priesthood.

In the early 1970s, Melba was called to be a seminary teacher in her stake. The stake president interviewed her for the calling, and he finished by asking if there was anything about Church doctrine that troubled her. Melba told him she didn't understand why their Black brothers and sisters couldn't hold the priesthood or receive the blessings of the temple.

"And he got a serious look," she recalled. "And he said, 'Well, that will come up.' And I said, 'I'm not on a soapbox about it; I just don't understand it. It seems like by now we should be able to welcome them to our faith.'"

I love her approach: she voiced her concerns and then continued moving forward, hoping things would change and that she would have more clarity. Melba did end up teaching seminary and loved it, but she continued to face friction within the Church.

The 1970s obviously brought up questions about the role of women in the home and Church. Melba loved to work outside the home and felt called to it, but she didn't appreciate how some men in the Church viewed her.

"I remember one time in the old San Dieguito Ward, I was standing out on the little porch, and I had my two boys with me," Melba recalled. "They had some of their friends with them, so there were about five kids there. And this man came out who was visiting our ward, and he said, 'That's what I like to see—an LDS mother surrounded by her children.' And I didn't mean to challenge him, but I just said, 'Oh, these aren't mine. *These* two are mine.' And he said, 'Oh,' and then he just strolled off in a huff." Melba got the feeling that having two children was not enough in this man's eyes.

On a later occasion, after she moved to Del Mar, she was called to be a Gospel Doctrine teacher. One man told the bishop he didn't think she should be able to teach the class because she didn't hold the priesthood.

"I didn't say a word to anybody," Melba said. "I just kept teaching and it never bubbled up again."

Another source of friction was the pushback Melba faced after Jerry stopped attending church shortly after their move to San Diego. Members of their ward would ask Melba why her husband wasn't active, and she couldn't understand why they would ask her such a personal question.

"A member came over one time and he said, 'I sure wish your husband would join the Church. You're such a faithful member.' I said, 'Oh, he's joined the Church," and he said, "He did? I thought he was just a nonmember.' Isn't that the worst way to say such a thing? It's like you don't count if you're not a member."

She told the man they had been married in the temple, and he asked her why Jerry was no longer active.

"Such a personal question from somebody. I don't understand that," Melba told me. "But I'm forgiving them. Because I know a lot of LDS people are raised in a very narrow corridor, and they aren't ready for a lot of things."

Melba continued to participate in the Church on her own for years, and she used the friction she faced to further develop her roots in the gospel and form connections with others.

One of the recurrent themes from the women I've interviewed is that we need a connection to other women, but sometimes their stories just aren't told. A lot of the women in this book did research to find women from the past who faced friction and were able to grow from it, and Melba did the same.

"Well, this is the good part of my story," Melba told me. "It made it all right for me to stay."

While teaching Sunday School one day and discussing Church leaders, a boy in her class asked her if she knew of any women in the history of the Church who had also played a vital role in their time. She mentioned Eliza R. Snow and Emma Smith, but he continued to ask her, "Who else?"

That put Melba on a project she called "The Elect Ladies of the 19th Century." She started researching and found records of wonderful Latter-day Saint women from the past: Ellis Reynolds Shipp, Lula Greene Richards, Patty Sessions, Jodi Wood, Susa Young Gates, and more.

"I started gathering my own set of women," Melba said. "Here's Ellis Reynolds Shipp, a famous physician who upgraded the midwife profession and went to medical school. Or Sarah Kimball, Minerva Teichert, Bathsheba Smith, and others."

One day when she was in Salt Lake City visiting family, Melba stopped by the Church historical department to see if she could get pictures of those women. She told the man working there what she was doing, and he was shocked—he had been working on slides of the same thing.

"And a week or so later in the mail I got all these slides of the women," Melba said. "For the Relief Society's birthday, I gave a talk about all these sisters, these 'elect ladies.'"

Melba started sharing her presentation in other wards and stakes, and the response was largely positive. While some people assumed Melba was trying to sow discord with her 'feminist' presentations, most thanked her for the work she had done.

"It really felt good for all of us," Melba shared. "I never knew women in the early Church went to medical school. I never knew they wrote poetry. I never knew about the *Woman's Exponent*. I didn't know they published their own newspaper. I didn't know they got to vote in 1870s. It was really exhilarating to be able to find their stories and then be able to tell them."

The women Melba found did not let friction slow them down to a stop; they used it to help them move faster. Melba found that learning about them gave her inspiration on how to deal with her own friction.

"It made me realize that they probably had a lot of doubts too, and yet they worked to their potential," Melba said. "They stayed in, they savored the good, and they had a compromise with the others, thinking: *It will change in time. It will change or it will be better.*"

As Melba shared what she learned, others had similarly positive experiences. The editor of *The San Diego Seagull*, a city-wide Latter-day Saint newspaper, saw Melba's presentation, and she liked it so much that she asked her to write a column for the paper. She did it for several years, and the column was a success.

Melba then started to consider contemporary "elect ladies," and looked at her peers. She started writing about women she knew who were divorced or single, because she had seen how people in the Church could treat them harshly.

"I wanted to bring those stories so we could talk about that," she said. "We shouldn't just enclose ourselves on a little shelf. We need to be welcoming and caring and supportive, even though every person isn't fitting a mold."

These modern stories were met with some backlash, and Melba was branded a "feminist"—a bad word to many people in those times. It was disappointing, but Melba looked to the examples of the women she had studied and was able to equalize her doubts with her faith-building experiences.

"It's always been a balancing act," she told me. "But I really believe; I'm a believer. And we have to educate each other."

One of the most destructive attitudes we see even today is that we oftentimes label people and then discount everything they say because of that label. This sometimes leads to inauthentic dialogue, especially with women. Melba's dedication to educating one another and balancing differing perspectives is an example we can all learn from.

"I weigh everything that comes out of my mouth when I'm around Church people," Melba said. "I try to avoid controversy. I want to keep focusing on what we can handle, what's good. And so that's the way I've been comfortable, and I think I'm liked and accepted."

Melba owes her sense of equilibrium to her mother and grandmother. Her grandmother taught her that the gospel was true and that Joseph Smith was a prophet of God, and Melba held on to that testimony when she felt shaky.

"I understand that we can't expect perfection of our leaders," she said. "We respect them, and they're wonderful, and most of them are very committed and sensitive, but some can be a little harsh at times. But every time I found myself drifting, I would just review the other things in the Church that had always been so positive, and I would say: *Joseph Smith is a prophet. And he was not perfect, nor ever claimed to be.*"

While Melba's grandmother taught her to build a strong testimony, her mother taught her to follow her own path. Her mother's example of hard work inspired Melba to do the same, both in her professional career and within the Church. That, plus Melba's own dedication to continued learning and growth, allowed her to navigate the ebbs and flows of friction in the Church.

"In any society, there's always something good and something bad," she said. "The good things were people, the blessings, the kindness that has been shown, the opportunities to serve, to tell my versions. . . . I have my views and they would come out. And I felt like I was welcomed."

Even today, when you walk into a room, Melba's spirit lights it up. She has found joy in her Church life and hasn't let any friction dull her brightness. She has blessed an untold number of students with her unbridled enthusiasm and her hope in Christ and continues to serve as an inspiration to continually seek learning and share what you learn.

Melba Kooyman was born in Ogden, Utah, and currently resides in Del Mar, California. Recently, Melba visited all seven continents to celebrate her seventieth birthday. She has two sons and seven grandchildren.

"I'm Going to Figure
This Out for Myself"

Christine Meaders Durham

||||||||||||||||||||||||||||||||

From becoming the first woman to serve in a judicial position in Utah to being appointed as the first female chief justice of the Utah Supreme Court, Christine Meaders Durham has spent her career shattering glass ceilings.

Both in and outside the courtroom, Christine has championed the cause of gender equality and education. She serves as a role model for countless women in Utah and beyond, proving that no societal norms or conventions can hold back a determined spirit. Her name is synonymous with a steadfast dedication to justice and balance, and those who know her personally can testify that she extends this devotion to all areas of her life, particularly with her family and with the Church.

Christine's relationship with the Church is marked by a commitment to seek personal revelation and combat inequality with the same intensity she does in the legal circuit. She has known members and leaders in the Church who have encouraged her to pursue her career, and she has encountered those who have tried to dissuade her from chasing her goals. She has faced people who were steadfast in prejudiced ways and others who were willing to have nuanced conversations with her. In all her experiences within the Church, Christine has balanced her ambivalent feelings toward it with grace and personal revelation.

"I just don't think God looks upon humans the way humans look upon each other," she told me when I asked her about prejudice within the Church. "I've been willing to say to myself, *They're just wrong*. And I'll let them be wrong if they don't require me to believe what they believe."[1]

Christine credits her parents for encouraging her to focus on education and pursuing her own goals. Her mother was unable to attend college, but never let go of her independent streak, which she passed on to Christine.

"Once when we were living in the Washington, D.C., area, we all were home for Wednesday night dinner," Christine recalled. "My mother looked around the table and said, 'Does anybody notice anything different around here?' We said, 'No, seems normal to us.' And she said, 'Well, that's good. I've been working for a couple of months now.' She had gone and found a job as a bookkeeper at a small business nearby, and she arranged her hours so that she was home before and after school."

Christine noted that she didn't think much of it at the time, but she now looks back and realizes that it was a huge deal for a Latter-day Saint woman in 1957 to go out and get a job. Her

---

1. (Durham 2023)

mother's example was part of what encouraged her to pursue an education, and Christine graduated from Wellesley College in 1967.

Other experiences in Christine's early life were equally formative. The Civil Rights movement opened her eyes to the discord that often existed between the ideals of the gospel and the reality of Church practices, particularly in regard to the ban on Black men holding the priesthood.

"What I see as the purity of the gospel, the ideal . . . of discipleship, and the idea of loving and not judging, and of embracing those who are in need, it's so hard to connect that to so much of what has happened in the Church," Christine shared.

Once during the late 1960s, Christine's bishop invited his father to speak in their ward's Sacrament meeting. When he did, he said several offensive and false things concerning race and the priesthood that stood against what Christine knew to be true about God's plan and His love for His children.

"I was as convinced as I've ever been about anything in the gospel that that was wrong," Christine said of the incident. "It was so anti-Christian—the gospel is a gospel of love. It was just sheer, pure prejudice about race."

She asked the bishop to not invite his father to speak in their ward again, although he continued to do so. Christine said that experience was the closest she's ever come to leaving the Church, but it forced her to contend with the dissonance surrounding race and the Church and taught her to trust personal revelation.

"I had to face the whole race thing, to grapple with it and get that answer," she said. "The visceral experience of the answer was that it wasn't right! I think that was a huge motivation for me, and I came to feel the same way about women's equality."

Many of the women I talked to, including Christine, first experienced friction within the Church because of the discrimination against black LDS members which they had a hard time as seeing as 'right'. For Christine, having to wrestle with it allowed her to learn how to struggle with something and recognize an answer. Most importantly, it would be a pattern she could use to identify answers in the future when she faced dissonance. She learned to allow herself space to hold her answer in her heart and mind and recognize that part of that answer was to stay in her faith community, even with the friction. I think the key for Christine is that she committed herself to staying in the Church—to experience the friction on occasion and learn from it. She also consistently looked for the good that participation could offer her.

Christine said that growing up on the East Coast was also beneficial to her understanding of the Church.

"All through college I was in Boston. I think it was missing a lot of the messages that were coming to young Latter-day Saints elsewhere," she said. "I had all these other influences coming from other places, and so I managed to create space for myself that allowed me to feel more independent about my choices."

"Create space"—those feel like two incredibly important words. When the world was created, Christ said, "We will go down, for there is space there . . . and we will make an earth" (Abraham 3:24). What strikes me is the principle of space: We need to have space to create something. Christine found and made space that allowed her to make independent choices, and her example can inspire each of us to create room for ourselves to make our own unique paths.

That created space led Christine to make the decision to study law while she was still attending college at Wellesley.

"I saw law as a means to righting wrongs," she said. "This was the impact of the Civil Rights movement on me."

She married George Durham during her junior year, and they both looked forward to pursuing their careers—hers in law and his in medicine—and starting a family. After they graduated, they moved to Arizona for the summer so George could work as a research fellow.

"I was very pregnant, and I got very depressed in the summer heat in Phoenix, and he got worried about me," Christine recalled. "He said, 'I think maybe you should think about starting law school.' I realized I was going to be changing diapers in the basement at our apartment while George was off finishing his biochemistry major. And so, I thought, *I'll go nuts. I will not be a good mother.*"

Christine wrote to the admissions board at Boston College and Boston University, and both responded and invited her to attend. The dean of Boston College, a Jesuit priest named Father Robert F. Ryan, personally spoke with Christine over the phone.

"He said, 'Bring the baby, we'd love to have you, and school starts September 15,'" Christine said. "The baby's due date was August 30, so I picked Boston College because they started later than Boston University."

Juggling law school, the baby, and George's school proved challenging, and Christine turned to her bishop for advice.

"I said, 'I'm worried about this, is this going to work out? Am I doing the right thing?'" she recalled. "The bishop said, 'Well, let me ask you a couple questions. So, how's the baby doing?' I said, 'Oh, she's fat and happy.' He asked, 'How is your marriage?' And I said, 'Well, we're doing fine. We still like each other when we see each other.' And then he said, 'How do you like law school?' I said, 'I feel like I belong there.' He said, 'You'll be fine.' And that was his counsel to me."

Supportive and sustaining experiences like the one Christine had with her bishop gave her experiences to fall back on later in her life, when people weren't as understanding. It also validated that her needs were as important as her family's.

"Some of it was pure self-preservation, as to why I had a career," Christine told me. "I've had depression most of my adult life, and I became very aware as a young adult that having meaningful work in my life, in addition to the incredibly meaningful work I was doing in my family, was essential to my health and well-being and probably survival."

While law school was difficult and both she and George had to pass up on some opportunities in order to spend more time with their family, Christine thrived. She transferred to Duke Law School when George was accepted to Duke Medical School, and she graduated in 1971 armed with knowledge and ambition.

After graduating from Duke, Christine and George chose to settle in Utah, and her arrival marked the onset of a radical change in the state's legal arena. Utah society in the 1970s was rather conservative and patriarchal, but Christine became part of a movement to enact progress. Nevertheless, the move was difficult; having lived outside of Utah her whole life, Christine faced a big cultural shock.

"I moved with my husband to Utah in 1973, and then spent the rest of the 1970s getting used to a Mormon-dominated society," she said. "Utah was quite a shock to me."

Christine recalls a Relief Society gathering she attended when she first moved to Utah that emphasized the cultural differences in feminism within and outside of the Church.

"They did a skit on bra burning," she told me. "It was angry and disrespectful. It made me feel like an outsider. It made me feel as if they disrespected some of the values, I'd held very dear from an early stage in my life: of fairness, equality, and opportunities for women."

Another experience Christine had soon after moving to Utah cemented her desire to pursue both motherhood and her career.

"I remember when we first got to Utah, I couldn't practice law for six months while I waited to take the bar," she said. "I used to walk our oldest down the block to cross the street to go to kindergarten, and there was a house a few houses down, and this neighbor would sit in her alcove in the bay window in the morning, in a bathrobe, just kind of a mess, slumped over, drinking a cup of coffee. I'd go by her, and for some reason I remember that whole vignette in gray, and it just had a visceral impact on me. I thought, *That's what will happen to me if I don't find a way to have these different components in my life.*"

In 1973, Christine began to sow the seeds of her distinguished career as a legal aid lawyer in Salt Lake City. Driven by her passion for justice and equality, she embarked on a challenging journey, demonstrating unusual mettle for a woman in her profession at the time.

Christine had experienced a combination of support and undermining from the Latter-day Saints she knew at her law school. While people like her bishop had been incredibly supportive, some of her classmates had suggested to her that she was taking up a seat that belonged to a man. She received similarly mixed responses to her career after moving to Utah.

"People at church in Utah would say, 'Is George's practice growing? Are you going to be able to stay home one of these days?'" she said. She would respond, "'Thanks, his practice is going fine, but I don't work for the money.' And that was something."

Christine knew herself well enough to recognize that for her, having a career and a family allowed for success and fulfillment in both. She and George both made sacrifices for that to happen, but as she said, they were happy as a family.

"I really was totally convinced not only that I would not do well, but that my children might not do well, if I experienced the sense of isolation and depression under the pattern that the Church set out for women and for families," Christine said. "It struck me as so restricted and so inconsistent with the notion of development. We're not here to put lids on our development. And at the same time, it's different for everyone, but it's got to be what's right for you."

This really solidifies for me how important it is to know yourself; to know what path you feel is best for you and then to take it. Focusing on development and growth allowed Christine to chart a path that didn't feel restrictive and allowed for the most growth. I also love that Christine pointed out that everyone must have their own development; each of our paths is unique by design. We need to focus on grace when looking at what others are doing in their life and assume they are doing what's right for them.

While there were certainly many points of friction between her and the Church, Christine told me that there were far more reasons for her to stay. In fact, the impetus for this book was Christine telling me over lunch one day that she was able to stay in the Latter-day Saint faith community even when there was conflict specifically because of the example of women who had come before her.

Susa Young Gates, George's great-grandmother, was one of those examples. She founded the *Young Women's Journal* and the *Relief Society Magazine* and was an advocate for women's rights. Christine sometimes carried around a letter that had been written by Susa's husband and mentioned the impact it had on her.

"The letter was about the opportunities that he had given to his wife, to build her life and to expand her influence and to serve across many arenas," Christine said. "I've treasured that letter forever because it was an example for me."

Susa's daughter and George's grandmother, Leah Eudora Dunford Widtsoe, was also a prolific author who earned advanced degrees. She was married to John A. Widtsoe, and it is widely claimed that they saw their marriage as a full partnership, which included both professional collaboration and raising their children.

"I think George's grandfather, John A. Widtsoe, was a really extraordinary human being—a scientist and academic—and his wife Leah was also a pioneer," Christine said. "She founded the home economics department at the university, she wrote books [. . .] and she was known as 'Mrs. Word of Wisdom.'"

Looking at women who had gone before Christine gave her strength, vision, and courage; it gave her permission to follow in their paths. The stories of these women gave her a sense of expansiveness in what she could do.

Christine was inspired by these women to use her own talents to address some of the friction she was feeling within the Church. When the Church came out in opposition to the Equal Rights Amendment with the rationale that passing individual laws addressing inequality would be preferable to a sweeping amendment, Christine used her skills to do just that.

"We went through the Utah codes page by page, and we did eliminate a huge amount of sex-based language in the Utah code, which made us feel really good," she said.

Christine did what she had the sphere of influence to do, and that allowed her to dissipate some of the discontent she felt on the issue of women's rights. Her dedication to justice and law was additionally rewarded with advancements in her career.

When she was appointed as a judge to the Third Judicial District in 1978 by Governor Scott Matheson, Christine became the first woman to serve in a general jurisdiction court in Utah. Despite the hurdles and undercurrents of resistance, she held her ground with exceptional grace and tenacity, proving that a woman's place can indeed be in the courtroom, behind the bench, wearing a judge's robe.

Four years later, in 1982, Christine's unwavering commitment to justice saw her ascend to the Utah Supreme Court, again as the first woman to do so. Here, she once again faced and overcame resistance and adversity, further highlighting her strength of character.

Throughout her career, participation in the Church gave Christine a source of community and friendship. In return, she has been a positive influence on many within the Church, serving as an example to other women just as Susa Young Gates and Leah Eudora Dunford Widtsoe are for her.

"I can't tell you how many times people who I don't even know, but people in my sphere, in my wards, and others, when I speak at conferences have come up to me and said, 'You give me so much hope. I watch what you're doing, and I realize there's so much that's possible,'" she said.

The pinnacle of Christine's trailblazing career came in 2002, when she was appointed Chief Justice of the Utah Supreme Court, a position she held with honor and distinction until her retirement in 2017. Her tenure was marked by landmark judgments, insightful interpretations of the law, and unshakeable integrity. Christine's leadership was instrumental in improving access to justice and advocating for judicial education.

Christine credits her ability to move forward and have a successful and fulfilling career while also remaining active and firm in the Church to the principle of personal revelation.

"What made it possible from the beginning to stay was to simply say, 'No, I'm going to figure this out for myself. I'm not going to compromise my values. I will try to be kind and beautiful,'" she said.

She also tributes her husband for seeking personal revelation alongside her and supporting her in her career and her spirituality. For Christine, having a partner to bounce things off of and get different perspectives from was incredibly helpful.

"I did my best to begin with, but we also did it together in our marriage, and that gave me a huge amount of confidence," she said. "As long as George was good, then I felt confident in being good myself."

She also realized that we get to pick our own narratives. How other people label you doesn't matter; it's what you decide yourself that's important. Christine also shows us that you can have friction in the community of the Church and have immense joy there at the same time.

"People were always saying to me, 'You can't be a Mormon and a feminist,' and I'm thinking, *That's for me to decide. Don't tell me what to do,*" she said. "The Church upsets me regularly, but I have also experienced a lot of good from it."

I love how Christine used a few benchmarks to be able to move forward in the friction she felt in the 1970s: Be kind and beautiful, don't compromise your values, and get personal revelation individually and as a couple to allow for confidence in your path.

"It's on us to get personal revelation for our own life. The Church leadership is invested in giving us principles to help us be more like Christ, but things get done by mere mortals in the implementation, and sometimes it isn't optimal or even inspired. We don't know so much here on Earth. We "see through a glass, darkly" (1 Corinthians 13:12), and we must remember that in our approach to everything we do."

I think Christine was articulating that she didn't have to believe that the way the messaging or programs were implemented was entirely how God would have done it if He had come down here and done it Himself. This is one of the challenges of dealing with uncertainties; so much of what we deal with is not definitive, and we crave clear answers.

"It's fascinating to me how much everything is very definitive sometimes, but on topics that are very nuanced," Christine noted. "I don't know why we have to be definitive on these things that are very nuanced. Let's just have a very nuanced discussion about it."

Christine added that being able to have these discussions and share different opinions is one of the best parts of being a member of the Church.

"The benefits of going to church are that you are with people who are never going to see things the same way as you," she said. "They have a different lived experience or different level of education. George says you're supposed to be in favor of different, and I feel like that's right."

It's interesting that the thing that often gives us friction—differences in perspective—is the very thing that can bring richness to our lives. Christine wanted to stay because she felt there was so much good, she could learn in the Church.

When I asked her what she would say to the rising generation, Christine outlined the necessity of assessing the level of misalignment and discomfort one feels within the Church or within their stake or ward. Some level of it is good for you;

sometimes it's annoying but doesn't necessarily affect your sense of self and actually enables you to grow.

I often wonder what kind of growth opportunities we miss when we eject ourselves just from a supreme annoyance. I loved how Christine looked at it. It's the same for any relationship, work situation, community situation: there will be friction. If we allow it to stop us, we are the ones who ultimately miss out on growth.

Even after her retirement, Christine remains a prominent figure in the legal community, inspiring the future generation of lawyers and judges. Her legacy, imprinted in the annals of Utah's legal history, serves as a testament to her courage, wisdom, and groundbreaking contributions. A woman of intellect, integrity, and indomitable spirit, Christine forever changed the landscape of Utah's judiciary, ensuring her place in the records of American jurisprudence.

||||||||||||||||||||||||||||||||||

Christine Durham resides in Salt Lake City Utah, and continues to practice law, she continues to fight for the rights of marginalized populations in her law practice. She enjoys chamber music, time with her husband George, and spending time with her children and grandchildren.

"I'm Staying Because I Found So Many Answers"

Susan Easton Black

When Susan Easton Black joined the faculty of Brigham Young University in 1978, she became the first female professor of religion in the 107-year history of the school. At the time, it was not a distinction she wanted.

"There were women in the more traditional areas: education, nursing, physical education, and women's sports," she recalled. BYU President Dallin H. Oaks "wanted to make sure there was a female full-time professor in every college. He found that there had not been a woman teaching religion, and so I was offered that opportunity. My knee-jerk reaction was 'no.'"[1]

I was surprised by this admission, and asked Susan why she didn't immediately jump at the chance.

---

1. (Black 2023)

"Well, a woman at that time who had a doctorate and was a Latter-day Saint was a rare commodity," she explained. "So, you stood out among all the others. It was a difficult time. I didn't want to be the fireside queen of the church."

But Susan has always stood out, even when she was young. She was driven to learn. She discovered in junior high that she had a photographic memory, and that propelled her further to pursue an education.

"When other friends were leaving high school and getting married," Susan said, "I was like, *Whoa, I'm going on. . . .* I love research. I love going to libraries. I like the smell of books, and I didn't want to leave this life with just being a name on a family group sheet."

She has gone far beyond that, having left her name on more than one hundred books and 250 articles. One of the preeminent experts on LDS Church history and Joseph Smith, Susan has lectured all over the world and inspired tens of thousands of Brigham Young students. She has three degrees, including a doctorate in educational psychology from BYU.

Breaking the glass ceiling in the 1970s, a time when women's roles were hotly debated in the Church and society at large, created quite a few friction points. Susan was a single mother with three children, and she faced criticism for her choices. She was in the spotlight, and it was often uncomfortable. But she had no doubts after one experience solidified for her the path she wanted to take.

"In 1978, I'm now teaching religion, and BYU is to send representation back to Nauvoo for the dedication of the Nauvoo Relief Society monument to women. And so, the crazy thing is, although I'm just an assistant professor and the lowest of the rank, I'm now being sent off to represent BYU."

The Church had created an incredible monument; at the time, it was the largest one in the world dedicated solely to women. The two-acre tribute tells the story of a woman, using sculptures and text from Ecclesiastes and Proverbs.

"As you go through, you can find a virtuous woman," Susan described. "Here she is as a youth; here she is courting; here she is as a mom; and then here she is as a woman in fulfillment, looking back. And it's like stepping into a Norman Rockwell painting—that was everything in my mother's era. I finally see the woman in fulfillment: she's at the end of this two-acre monument, and she's got a quilt over her lap that no doubt she made. I wouldn't consider doing that! She looks back, and she is fulfilled at this life of daughter, wife, mother—and happy."

Susan had a sudden epiphany at that moment.

"The impact for me was the one statue with the woman who was wearing the short skirt, and what I thought was so amazing is that she is sculpting, and what she is sculpting is her face—her very own face, but it's her own face when she's older, when she is in fulfillment. It's her own face of what she wants to do in her life. And suddenly I thought, *I relate to this*. I actually do want and appreciate being a daughter, a wife, a mother. But I also want to also use my talents and develop my face so that I can fulfill in some small and major ways my potential."

Fulfilling her potential, however, was not an easy path.

"You can imagine, when I first started at BYU there were questions as I came to the meetings," she recalled. "'Are you here to take notes? I like your perfume and your pink dress.' It took a while for them to accept me and make me feel like I fit in. . . . But the thing that saved me is background and talent."

When friction becomes unbearable, there is always a risk of letting it slow you down to a stop. Susan reflected on why she didn't let that happen during those turbulent times.

"Why would I stay?" she said. "You know, I think it's difficult to be an individual in a large organization and yet maintain your individual desires and succeed, and not move with the norm. I've had some pretty hard moments where I'm like, maybe I should quit working at BYU. But what has really guided me—that perhaps has been the most helpful through all of it—has been my patriarchal blessing. I'd see my peers and have them question at church what I was doing and think perhaps I should change. And it caused me to question it. But again, I would go back to that blessing and go, 'Well, here's me!'"

For many, a patriarchal blessing can be a real source of inspiration and identification of traits and paths that could become available. It allows us to see ourselves in a new light and can give us a sense of who we were and who we can be. Looking at her patriarchal blessing in a new way was key, Susan said.

"One thing I did with my blessing that really helped through this kind of tumultuous time, as I was trying to make a sculpture of my own face, was to take my blessing apart a little bit: Here are my promises. Here are my blessings. Here are the specifics I'm to be doing; my personal part. And then here are my warnings. . . . For a woman to move forward in the '70s, or even today, and to be who their Heavenly Father wants them to be, it takes stamina, it takes determination. It takes a lot of grit. You cannot be just 'OK.' So, I've tried to be in my life like Captain

Moroni: He only went into battles that he knew he could win, and most battles aren't worth it."

Some of those battles came because of questions Susan had.

"You know, everyone comes to a point where they've got questions about the Church, right?" she said. "I decided incredibly young that I would ask questions, say, in a Sunday School class. Actually, the first time the bishop ever called me in—and I wish I could say it was the last—was to tell me to leave my scriptures at home and give the Sunday School teacher a chance."

Susan decided this wasn't a battle worth fighting. She realized that raising her hand in Sunday School was pointless when the teacher had no idea what the answer was.

"So, I started a notebook, and I started writing all the questions I had about the Church," Susan recounted. "Rather than throw the baby out with the bathwater, I just wrote question after question. Everything that bothered me. Another question. Another question. So, I'm now fifty-plus years beyond that event, and every Christmas I take out my old book, and I try to see how many questions I've been able to answer. And so, I'm now, I don't know, at maybe 92 percent answered."

But despite the struggle to find answers, despite the isolation of being a female professor at BYU when so few women were on the faculty, despite the friction Susan faced every week at church, she stayed. Why?

"I know Jesus is the Christ. I know Joseph Smith was a prophet. I've found those answers for myself," she explained. "Sometimes I'll have people say to me, 'I'm leaving the Church because I have so many questions.' I go, 'I'm staying because I found so many answers.'"

Of course, getting answers often takes years, but Susan found that in the meantime, remembering her previous experiences receiving answers kept her continually seeking for more.

"I think a lot of times people are too quick to throw out the sacred ground they've captured," Susan reflected. "Why did you stop searching for the answer? And why did you allow questions on the internet—that were not even your questions—trouble you? . . . Why did you allow that to destroy something that you have literally built up through sacred moments of knowledge and experience? To let it just go as if it is a thing of naught when you have had these amazing experiences. But if you don't write them down, the experiences vanish."

Decades of seeking answers and encountering friction have equipped Susan with perspective and counsel that I found truly insightful. She helped me realize that centering too much on one question can affect your spiritual eyesight—anything else becomes out of focus.

"You have to be moving forward, and every day really has to be your best day, because it's the only day you've got, right?" Susan said. "Questions and concerns and difficulties—if they crowd the day, then what good have you done for someone else? I have had concerns, including concerns today. I move forward in the realm of things that I can do, and I personally can change. . . . But you know, sometimes you just really don't have power or influence over an issue. If you can't make that change, why labor when there are so many other things you could be doing? It's an obstacle if you don't keep moving forward, and then wait patiently on the Lord. I think, unfortunately, when you do that, when you glom onto one thing, then you forget the big picture. Don't lose the beautiful picture in minutia. There will be new issues that will come again and again. And if you're not in the position to make change, you just need to wait for the moment."

Susan's stellar legacy is undisputed. Among her many accolades, Susan received the Karl G. Maeser Distinguished Faculty Lecturer Award in 2000. Not only was she chosen out of 1,700 faculty, she was also the first woman *and* the first religion professor to receive the prestigious award.

"You know, when I was a kid, my mother hoped—and I did too—that I would become Miss Universe," she quipped. But "the thing that was the most exciting is that my picture is on the wall in the BYU library. Now, it's not exactly what my mother—or even I—had hoped. But I think years from now, I will have left something for others to build on."

IIIIIIIIIIIIIIIIIIIIIIIIIIIIIII

Susan Easton Black was born in Long Beach, California, in 1944. She had three sons whom she raised as a single parent until 1986, when she married Harvey Black. He passed away in 2011, and in 2012 she married George Durrant. She currently resides in Provo, Utah. Susan holds a bachelor's degree in political science from Brigham Young University, a master's degree in educational counseling from the University of California, and an Ed.D in educational psychology from BYU.

"Peace"

Nora Mercedes Cummings

||||||||||||||||||||||||||||||||||

Nora Cummings radiates an unmistakable zest for life, her laughter and quick wit lighting up any room she enters. Her story is a tapestry of resilience and joy, intricately woven with moments of hardship that have deepened her commitment to peace and shaped her boundless empathy.

The narrative of Nora's life began in 1953 Guantanamo, Cuba, a land cradled by an azure bay located 500 miles south of Havana and watched over by the enduring presence of a U.S. Naval base. It was in this dichotomy of beauty and political complexity that Nora's foundational values were shaped. Her maternal lineage, replete with education and affluence, and her mother's relentless pursuit of knowledge set a formidable example.

"My mom was such a great role model and a great example. My mother lived to learn. My mother had PhDs in Chemistry and Physics and degree in Pharmacology. And she was amazing at music . . . she was totally ahead of her time." Recounts Nora with pride, describing a hallway in their Florida home adorned with a legacy of academic achievements, a silent testament to her mother's intellectual prowess and a monument to the pursuit of excellence.[1]

Nora's father's story contrasts starkly with her mother's privilege, his life an odyssey from humble beginnings to becoming the highest-ranking Cuban civilian at the US base. His multilingual abilities and his fervent fight for democracy in Cuba during tumultuous times painted a backdrop of resilience and determination that would come to define Nora's own spirit.

Nora reflects, "In Cuba, there were really two classes—you had money, or you did not. And my sister and I were old enough to see that the difference between how I lived, and the way others lived. My Parents believed that Cuba needed some reformation, the social division between the people of Cuba was vastly different and a middle class was needed. My dad was very involved with that. Trying to have different leadership for the country that was really going to change things and was going to stabilize things."

Political tides turned in the late 1950s with the success of Fidel Castro, and his subsequent allegiance to the USSR. Once a Castro believer, Nora's father was now branded a Castro traitor. He attempted a daring escape for political asylum at the Guantanamo Naval Base. The sight of his bullet-riddled car on Cuban television was a harrowing moment of truth for a six-year-old Nora, one that would be softened only by the reassurance of his safety, by a late-night call from the U.S. Government.

---

1. (Cummings 2024)

During this time of anxiety in Cuba, an event happened that would commence Nora on a path to learn empathy. After what seemed like an interminable wait, which was in reality 18 months, her mother, herself, and her two sisters had received papers to fly from Cuba to Miami to reunite with their father, who had established himself in Miami and continued to work for the US government. Nora recounts, "It was a short flight from Havana to Florida, but for my sister and I it never happened. Just before the plane was to take off Cuban government officials came onto the plane followed by my grandfather to tell us that my sister and I could not leave due to paperwork issues. My mother was perplexed as she knew that all the paperwork was correct. My grandfather counseled her to go because she had been away from my dad for so long, she could not work, and she was being followed all the time. She agreed to leave but with the promise from her father that he would put us on the plane the next day to Florida. That plane was delayed by 5 years."

Scarcity marked the 'left behind' period in Cuba, education and food were non-existent. Being left behind in Cuba was foundational for Nora, she was imprinted by with the relentless optimism of her parents, "My mother and most Cubans are very optimistic. There's a glass is never empty attitude, not even when its half full or completely empty. My mom would say, "This too shall pass. We are living in a not the best moment, but it is not going to define us, we're not going to forget it, but it's going to make us stronger." The foundation of this time created empathy for the young Nora. "I learned empathy during this period of my life, today when I hear of the struggles of people around the world that have lost family members, their homeland, their language, their way of life, or that have been separated from loved ones, I pray for them."

Amid the echoes of her Catholic upbringing, Nora's spiritual sojourn was met with dissonance and yearning for a more personal communion with the Divine. "I was thankful that I was raised with faith and a desire to follow the commandments, to pray and be obedient, but I had questions. I always believed that the Trinity was actually three different beings. I also wanted my own prayers. I did not believe that I needed a prayer book or that my prayers, to be heard, needed to be through one of the many saints in the Catholic Church."

Life in the United States brought up a stark contrast, in Cuba she was able to attend a private catholic school, but monetary constraints didn't allow this in the US. In Cuba, her family had paid for school for many students, and nobody did that for them in Miami, which "didn't sit well" with Nora regarding her Miami Catholic community.

Within the embrace of the LDS Church that Nora found a deep source of joy and peace that anchored her life. An invitation for 16-year-old Nora to a midweek church activity became the fulcrum for the rest of Nora's life. Missionary discussions became a regular part of her life for over a year. While learning was encouraged at home, fully joining the Church was a different matter entirely. Even without permission to be baptized, Nora's path in the Church was marked with unwavering commitment to sharing the gospel, an endeavor she undertook with her sister as they worked alongside missionaries to rekindle the flames of faith in their community. "We would go out with the sister missionaries and give lessons to them, we would bear testimony, we would talk about the Book of Mormon. We had callings and we were actively working in the Church. The Spanish branch was an amazing branch with amazing members and amazing people."

Without being official members of the Church, Nora and her sister ended up teaching and facilitating the baptism of about six of their best friends. Her father's blessing to join the LDS Church despite the initial hesitance, was given because he watched her continued commitment and dedication while she wasn't allowed to join.

"My Father said, 'You have decided to fall in love with what I consider one of the strictest religions in the planet.' And he said, 'I know a lot of good LDS people . . . your mom and I have talked about it, and we are wondering if you are embracing too much of what you consider good and great in your new country the United States.' The Catholic religion was so foundational to who we were, where we came from and our ancestors. My dad also understood about commitment and passion for beliefs, and he had seen this in my sister and me. So, my dad said, 'It's going to break your grandparents' heart. But I'm going to give permission for you guys to be baptized.' We could not believe it. Obviously, nobody showed up at our baptism. Driving home, I thought our house was on fire. Because my grandma had lit candles to every saint in the Catholic calendar asking for protection and forgiveness."

Education, once a given, became a privilege that she and her family fought to maintain amidst scarcity and upheaval. Nora commenced college in Florida but eventually relocated to the

University of Utah, and the heartland of her adopted faith, presented a new set of challenges. A move to the homogenous enclave of Bountiful Utah precipitated by her marriage in 1975 brought a new landscape to understand. In Utah, Nora's vibrant Cuban heritage initially set her apart, but it also lent her the strength to stand firm in her convictions. Her work ethic and her commitment to family and faith were pillars that supported her as she navigated the complexities of a new cultural landscape. The friction she experienced only served to sharpen her resolve and deepen her understanding of herself and her place within the tapestry of her community.

She stuck out from the 'norm' with her bold colors, her lipstick, her clothes, her accent, the color of her hair and skin and her way of being. She related quite a few incidents where her 'cubaness' didn't fit into the mostly homogenous intermountain west landscape of the early 1970s.

"Along this journey of adjustment, I have relied on the knowledge that I was a daughter of God loved just the way I was. What others have perceived as challenges and friction, I have seen as another opportunity to go to Heavenly Father with these questions as it pertains to topics that might cause friction, such as Blacks and the priesthood and women in leadership positions but not ordained to Priesthood offices. My covenants have blessed myself and my family. And I have seen mountains move because of the prayer of a faithful woman."

In 1981 after three beautiful children in the span of 5 years, Nora felt her family was complete. Conversations with family, friends and neighbors made her wonder if something was wrong with her since at 26, she thought she was done with childbearing. "I remember speaking to my mother reminded me that 'you cannot immerse yourself into something that you lose sight of who you are." Consulting her doctor about a physical ailment she was experiencing, surprisingly the doctor told her, "You are trying too hard to fit into a mold that you are not meant to be in. Be yourself." Nora took those words as meaning that the size of your family should not be determined by others, but is best left to you, your husband, and the Lord.

A time of quite introspection resulted, where foundational questions of who she was, what she wanted in life, and what God wanted from her needed to be resolved. This exercise in quite reflection cemented her courage and focus to move through friction for the rest of her life.

Nora's professional journey was equally marked by determination and the desire to connect with others. "Why did I like to work? I liked to be around people. I'm a people person. I love to know people's background, culture, vocation, and hobbies. There is so much satisfaction in putting heels on and going and learning something new. Doing something for your own, contributing something, may not be as satisfying as raising kids. But being with coworkers improved my mental health." Nora always found that being around other people, and engaging with the world helped her in all aspects of her life including being a better mother.

Although Nora trained as a Special Ed teacher, she was never drawn to that profession She found herself doing part-time jobs in the retail industry that eventually led to a storied career at Nordstrom. She started a few days a week, but then there was a meteoric rise that concluded when she retired at 60 as Executive Vice President at Nordstrom, responsible for most of the Southwest. Along her career path, she managed stores, was a buyer, and made several moves with Nordstrom to different locations including Utah, Northern California, Texas, and landing in San Diego as her final relocation. She retired from Nordstrom and within about 6 months realized she missed the stimulation of problem solving, mentoring others, goal setting and impacting for good. Today she is VP of Impact and Retail at a great company in San Diego and sees herself always working and mentoring others.

Her career at Nordstrom was not just a job but a mission field where she applied the principles learned from the Church to her leadership style. The empathy and understanding she cultivated through her life's challenges allowed her to lead with compassion and inspire those around her. "What I have learned from the church is so invaluable. I got a figurative PhD by being a member of the church. If you go to my desk right now, you will see a plaque that says, I teach people good principles, and then they govern themselves."

During the 1970s and early 1980s Nora felt some of the friction within the LDS church around working mothers. She reminisced around a couple of particular episodes throughout her career that outlined the narrative of friction for those women choosing to work and participate in the LDS faith. After one General Conference when it was reiterated that women should be in the home and not working, Nora remembered showing up the very next day at the Nordstrom in Salt Lake City and a number of women were waiting to speak to her. They immediately asked her if she would be quitting and if she wasn't did that mean the Prophet wasn't speaking to her. "I told them, he was speaking to everyone. But now it's up to us to take it to a Heavenly Father and say, 'These are the reasons why I work . . . and get your own answer. There isn't a one size fits all."

Nora insists that "I think that Prophet was saying just be mindful of the amount of time we devote to the things that matter most, and I admit that I was actually a better mother because I worked. And my kids will agree with this. I have the conviction and have the reassurance that I have made the right decision to work."

She recalls, in the early 1990s sitting in a Sunday School class in the Northern California, flanked by successful career women. A priesthood leader said "It's really hard for me to be in this room, when I see some sisters that are making five times more than what their brethren do. It is very unbalanced and un-fair. In some cases, some of these men are out of a job. And they have a family to support." Nora recounted "We talked about it afterward (the other women). I think we all felt the same way in the gospel doctrine class. And the thing is that everybody knew that he was talking about us. It was one of those things that was inappropriate and insensitive and a bit sharp. But he has his free agency. He could say whatever he wants. Did it hurt? Absolutely, for a second. But it didn't change anything." She felt that there are always times in the ward where somebody can sabotage your testimony, but if you focus on the peace and joy of the gospel, that interconnectedness that sometimes causes friction gives opportunities for joy and learning.

As the narrative of her life unfolded, Nora's capacity for empathy, honed through years of facing and overcoming adversity, became a central theme. Whether dealing with cultural dissonance, reconciling her faith with her upbringing, or finding her place in a new country, Nora's journey has been one of seeking and finding peace through understanding and love.

Today, Nora Cummings stands as a testament to the enduring power of faith and the strength that comes from a life lived with purpose and passion. Her story is a beacon of hope and a reminder that friction can be the force that polishes our character and hones our capacity for compassion. Her legacy is one of joy, resilience, and an unwavering commitment to the principles that have guided her every step of the way.

||||||||||||||||||||||||||||||||

Nora Cummings resides in San Diego, California with her husband. She continues to be incredibly active in her community, spending a lot of energy moving forward the interfaith dialogue in her area. She spends time mentoring young women earlier in their career in her 'free' time. She also spends time with her children and grandchildren.

"I Knew the
Path I Was On"

Marilyn Phillips

‖‖‖‖‖‖‖‖‖‖‖‖‖‖‖‖‖‖‖‖‖‖‖‖‖‖‖‖‖

Friction is no respecter of persons; it appears in different ways for everyone. For Marilyn Phillips, she faced friction in the Church not because of her successful career, but because of her status as a single mother after a painful divorce. While her path in life didn't always turn out as she expected, she nevertheless strove forward with courage and faith. When faced with curveballs, she learned to reevaluate her previous plans and seek inspiration from the Spirit.

Marilyn was born into a Latter-day Saint family and grew up in Provo, Utah, where her father taught at Brigham Young University. She described her childhood as a happy one; she never experienced friction in the Church regarding her gender or her ambitions, and her experiences with leaders and family members were positive.

"I was never made to feel like I didn't have a place in the Church or a place in the world because I was a woman," she told me recounting her growing up experience. "Rather, I felt that I was capable. I was smart. I could do whatever I wanted to do if I was willing to work at it."[1]

Marilyn began attending college in 1969, a time of great change in the world. While her father was concerned about a potentially turbulent future for the country, Marilyn said it was an exciting time for her and others in her generation.

"We were going to start taking over society and running the country and managing things and moving things ahead, and there was no fear or trepidation," she said. She recalls telling her father, "'You don't need to worry about us. We can manage all of this. Wonderful things are opening.'"

Marilyn told me she's sure young people today feel the same way; even with all the upheaval in the world, there are opportunities for growth and positivity. Marilyn expressed hope that today's generation can approach this transformation with the same excitement she did. She has faced several unexpected twists in her life, and she handled them all by proactively determining her path and involving Heaven in her decisions.

Marilyn's life seemed to be going as planned: she got married in 1969, graduated with an English degree, and started graduate school. She began teaching freshman English, which had been her dream for some time.

---

1. (Phillips 2023)

"I always saw myself as teaching," she said. "I love teaching. It was not a hard thing for me; I was creative, I like talking, I love teenagers."

Marilyn considered teaching college classes, but her husband got a job that relocated their young family to California. Marilyn was content staying at home and raising their children, but after her second child was born, the life she had planned for started to drift out of her reach.

"It became really apparent to me that our marriage was not going to survive, because of addiction and infidelity on my former partner's part," she said.

Marilyn began to recognize that she couldn't stay with her husband, but it was difficult for her to leave, not just because of religious reasons, but no-fault divorce lack of ability for women to have access to checking accounts and credit were recent hurdles that were just starting to be overcome. She started working again in order to achieve financial independence.

"It took five years for me to be ready to divorce him and to leave the marriage, and during that time I was the financial breadwinner," she said. "I did not go to work because I needed it for my self-esteem or that I was bored at home or that we were going to get a big boat. It was survival."

Marilyn could no longer be a stay-at-home mother, nor did she want to return to teaching. She wanted a solid career; she didn't want to be anyone's assistant.

"I'm very logical in my thinking, so I just worked it out: *What do I want my life to look like? What is going to be able to give me enough financial reward?* And that was just kind of how I started," she said.

Marilyn turned to people in her ward for advice. She made appointments with several who had successful careers and asked them for guidance. They helped her identify potential career paths and opportunities, and one set up an interview for her with the president of a savings and loan bank. She got the job.

"First I was in management training, then a branch manager, and then I ran a department and ended up coming to Las Vegas and working for Bank of America," she said. "I graduated from a savings and loan to a commercial bank."

While Marilyn acknowledged that the Church made it clear that it was important for women to stay at home, she didn't feel conflicted about choosing to work. She attributes that to being close to the Holy Ghost and having confidence in the answers she got through that line of communication.

"I just didn't see that the Church narrative applied to me because of the circumstance I was in," she said. "I felt the connection with the Spirit and the approval of the Holy Ghost very strongly in my decisions. I knew the path I was on and that what I was doing was approved and was right."

Marilyn added that her ability to compartmentalize helped her avoid stress around the matter.

"If it could have been different, that would have been wonderful, but because it wasn't what I could do, I chose not to concern myself with it," she said.

Marilyn told me that she knows a lot of women her age who now regret that they didn't seek the same spiritual guidance in their paths. They feel that they did what they thought they were supposed to do—what they had specifically been told to do—but now, they are unsure whether it was the right course.

"I see a conflict with women my age who now look back and say, 'I wonder what I could have done,'" Marilyn said.

As she recounted this, what struck me as the difference between Marilyn and some of her peers was that she had confidence in her decisions because she relied on investigating what the prophetic counsel meant to her by assuming she could check with God to understand what the specifics were for her life. Because she had complete assurance that she had taken the path God wanted her to, she never had to look back and wonder what she could have done instead. I think some of her peers didn't necessarily use the opportunity to work with Heaven to figure out what path they could have taken, whether that was to remain at home and do the essential work there or to work outside the home by starting a career. Because they didn't have that spiritual confirmation, they don't have the confidence that the path they took was the best option.

Listening to Marilyn's story clarified for me that a key aspect of our development is learning to obtain a confirmation of our decisions by making them in conjunction with God.

"I keep using the term 'self-confidence,' but I think it's self-confidence in your understanding with the Lord," Marilyn told me. "Not that you're 100 percent on anything, but that you're working and you're moving forward. You keep going, it all continues, and as it does, it just builds more of a reservoir within you that you continue to move forward with."

While this confidence blessed Marilyn to avoid experiencing conflict within the Church regarding her career, friction is inevitable in this life. For her, it surfaced in another area—specifically, in being divorced in a faith with such an emphasis on traditional families. It made it difficult for her to keep going to church after her divorce.

"I had been the Relief Society president in our ward, and my ex-husband was the former Young Men's president," she said. "Then everything went crazy with my marriage, and it was quite public in the ward because of my husband's actions."

One Saturday soon after the divorce, Marilyn was sitting in her bedroom, dreading having to face her ward the next day.

"I have to take these three kids to church, and I thought, *they don't want to go, and it's going to be a struggle*," she said.

She imagined how people would ask her where her husband was, or tell her how sad they were for her, and she couldn't bear it.

"And I just thought, *I can't keep doing this. I cannot keep doing this*," she said.

In that moment, Marilyn decided to step away from the Church for a while. She figured people would be so happy when she came back that they wouldn't ask any uncomfortable questions, and she'd be able to skip this painful time. After all, she knew the Church was true; why did she have to keep attending?

Marilyn told me that as soon as she thought that she heard a voice say, "Yes, but if you don't go, how will they [your children] know? And at that moment, I realized that I was going to continue going so I could teach them what I knew, and so they never had to question what I believe in."

We all have moments in our lives where we reach a crossroads. For Marilyn, she used that crossroads to strengthen her faith in and commitment to the Church. It was still hard to go to church the next day and the Sundays after that, but she focused on her relationship with the Savior instead of others' perception of her.

"The biggest friction I had in the faith community was with the idea of being a single woman, once I was divorced," she shared. "But I didn't let it bother me because I had enough confidence in where I was, what I was doing, that it was OK."

The people Marilyn cared about the most understood her, and she realized that it didn't matter what anyone else thought. She continued to grow her faith, little by little, through the small and simple steps of the gospel.

"I've always known that God was real, and I say, 'always' because there was no 'aha' moment," she told me. "I just had experiences that allowed me to continue to grow and to make mistakes and to repent and to feel that joy, and all the learnings that came from that just developed more."

Marilyn told me she's grateful for the guidance from the Spirit that helped her through her divorce, raising her three sons as the sole breadwinner and parent and gave her the strength to withstand the friction she felt within the Church.

"It's what I know. It's what I believe," she said. "It's what I've sacrificed for. It's how I've raised my children.

Marilyn emphasized the importance of continuing to work on your testimony.

"I love learning and I love gaining more knowledge and insight," she said. "The more I learn and the more layers I see, the more I recognize the truthfulness and the complexity and the beauty of the gospel."

Marilyn's commitment to the intricacies of the gospel, of life, of the principle of friction, and of our own individual paths is inspiring. Her example of seeking personal revelation and adapting her path when necessary has encouraged those who know her to follow her example, and I hope sharing her story inspires even more.

‖‖‖‖‖‖‖‖‖‖‖‖‖‖‖‖‖‖‖‖‖‖‖‖‖‖‖‖

Marilyn Phillips lives in the Boise, Idaho, area today with her husband, Ned. They were married in 2000 after Ned Phillips moved into her ward in Las Vegas, a newly single father. They are the parents of a combined seven children.

"To Be Blessed"

Mercedes Lorenzana

|||||||||||||||||||||||||||||

Mercedes Lorenzana's life reflects a deep sense of gratitude, a thread that runs through both her joys and challenges. She sees each experience as a blessing, guided by the Lord's hand. Born in Lima, Peru, in 1944, Mercedes grew up in a close-knit Catholic family that valued faith and education. Her mother, an English teacher, made sure her children were bilingual, opening doors for future opportunities. After graduating high school and completing a two-year business program in 1961, Mercedes's bilingual skills and expertise in shorthand quickly set her apart in the workforce.

Mercedes's career took a significant leap when she joined the staff at ESAN, a graduate business school in South America set up by Stanford in the early 1960s. Not long after, she saw an ad for a position with the Pan American Health Organization (PAHO), part of the United Nations, and applied. Soon, she was in the United States, excelling in a high-pressure role supporting the director, who was also Peru's former vice president.

Mercedes thrived in this environment for 17 years, balancing the demands of the job with her knack for connecting with people from diverse backgrounds. After her time as executive support, she moved to PAHO's Personnel Department, where her mentorship and advocacy for employee development made a lasting impact. After 34 years, she retired from PAHO at the age of 55.

Mercedes credits her faith and resilience for carrying her through challenging times. Her early experiences in Peru instilled a fierce determination, which helped her navigate life in the United States while staying true to her roots.

Mercedes' family of origin propelled her to seek out a fuller spiritual 'home'. Her loving father was a journalist at the most impressive newspaper in Peru and was from an upper middle-class family that owned racing horses. Her household experienced the rarity of divorce in a devoutly catholic family when she was 17 years old, because "liking horses and drinking was not a good recipe for a happy marriage." Amid the backdrop of change that she found solace in the teachings of a new church; a friend told her "There is a new church in the neighborhood. Do you want to come and listen to the missionaries?" When she went "they started talking to me about the gospel and then I saw the families and I saw even though some were poor families, they were happy, and I was seeking for happiness. And for me, I loved it. Instantly, I said, oh, this is what I want." She immediately started attending, and taught classes, all while still not being baptized. She characterized that there she "found peace, happiness and that's what it was for me."[1]

---

1. (Lorenzana 2024)

It wasn't just that she saw families happy regardless of their socio-economic status, it was the combination of the people, the Book of Mormon, and the doctrine "When you do the things that are right? Who's your companion? The Holy Ghost. And he's the one who has accompanied me all my years and I always try to do what is right and that's what I think gives me peace and happiness because really, I found happiness in the church and the gospel." Her journey to conversion unfolded over four years, a time spent learning and serving, until at last, she gained the permission she needed to take the step of baptism.

Her move to the United States marked the beginning of a new chapter, with the LDS Church playing a central role. The day after her arrival, she immersed herself in the activities of the Washington DC singles ward. The rapid growth of Spanish-speaking members moved the 'class' to a 'group' within the congregation, with Mercedes's inherent leadership creating a weekly Mutual version that worked for their cultural needs. All ages, 12–99 attended on Wednesday night, which just increased the community closeness and membership resulting ultimately in the 'group' becoming a Spanish Branch. This was quite a departure from the English-speaking congregations, that were more divided by age, and sex.

Mercedes took great joy when, after a few years, the next Branch President was a Hispanic member. She mentioned that "attending the little branch was beautiful and wonderful." Mercedes along with her husband, Marco, demonstrated what she had throughout her career and life, which was a penchant for solving problems, including others, and shepherding other Hispanics to a better place.

Sometime later in, the late 1970s, one of the Apostles came to a big conference in the DC area, and announced the eventual dissolution of Spanish branches, a directive that seemed like a death knell to their close-knit community. She said of the dissolution "I felt like I was going to die. How could it be?"

Quite unexpectedly for Mercedes the situation was remedied, by having to immediately serve in leadership callings in their new ward which brought a sense of learning, belonging and gratitude. To hear Mercedes, she was blessed in every experience in all wards, because she always looked at it from a perspective of gratitude and learning.

All things ebb and flow, and the Spanish branches were later reconstituted, with her husband serving as a high councilman over the ward and eventually as the bishop. At this point she didn't want to take her children out of the "American" programs in her geographic ward where her children had friends living around them, so she kept her children in their original ward, and she attended both. As usual, she leveraged tried and true methods for success in the Hispanic ward, but tailored to fit the unique needs of the Spanish congregation.

So many threads have created Mercedes tapestry, one of the faith promoting experiences for her during a span of 4 decades was her battle with brain aneurysms. Her first brain aneurysm occurred when she was 5 months pregnant with her youngest daughter. Each occurrence precipitated brain surgery, and long painful recoveries that included relearning speech, and physical abilities. As many things in her life, this became another stone in her foundation over and over as she went through the experience 4 different times with 7 years in between. "I think because of all the health challenges that I had made me strong and that made me come so close to HIM because what did I do when after my operations they put me in the ICU for many days, all alone? I prayed to him all day and learned to pray in such a way that I became close to him. He is my companion."

Her professional and spiritual journeys were not without their moments of dissonance, especially during the era when church narratives seemed to conflict with her lived reality. Lived reality in the Spanish congregations was that women were all working at least one if not more jobs. It was never discussed in those congregations that women shouldn't work—even though that was the 'official' narrative. Her experience was anything but that in the non-Spanish congregations. Mercedes recalls the poignant moments in her geographic ward Relief Society when the counsel of the time clashed with her own convictions. "I remember trying not to pay attention, because I was not happy with [it]. . . . When I went to Relief Society, I'd have a baby in my arms and they would be saying, 'Women should stay home and raise their children, that's what you should do.' I would listen to that, and I would get up with my baby in my arms and leave the room. I didn't say anything, but I was not happy."

Her response was not one of confrontation but of quiet resolve and prayerful introspection. "I started praying a lot to the Lord then, and I thought that at home I was doing Heavenly Father's work, but at work as well. In talking with my husband, we decided that me working was a something between me, my husband, and the Lord. With the support of my husband and family members, together we were able to raise our family the way we felt was right for us."

Mercedes's life has been a symphony of roles: a mother at home, a professional in the international sphere, and a beacon of support in her community. She and her husband orchestrated a home where family dinners were sacrosanct, a time for connection, reflection, and shared dreams. Stepping into retirement at 55 wasn't about slowing down—it was a thoughtful choice driven by a deep spiritual impression. Reflecting on the decision, she relates, "I know it was Heavenly Father and the Holy Ghost they were telling me that's what I needed to do because people thought it was silly for me to quit at that time."

Education, for Mercedes, was a cornerstone of empowerment. She tirelessly championed the pursuit of higher learning within her family and the Hispanic community at large, often echoing to her children, "dad and I work, and work hard. Your job is school. You have to get good grades, that is your job."

Her advocacy extended beyond her immediate family as she created pathways for Hispanic youths to envision and attain a collegiate future. Tours of educational institutions and motivational speeches and uncovering the little understood world of financial scholarship and aid, were tools she leveraged. She would also go throughout her area, talking to principals, teachers and students encouraging the Hispanic students, "You can be whoever you want to be, but you have to start, and you can do it. You can be whoever you want to be, but you have to study."

She recognized that to support of her LDS Hispanic community she would also need to go upstream to the source and talk directly to parents, "Learn English, learn how to drive, so you can get better jobs, support your children in school, check their homework, tell them they have to do their homework . . . and the importance of education."

Over the years Mercedes helped hundreds of Hispanic youths attend college, both monetarily and inspirationally. Compelled to follow this mission because "it's personal to me, because I am Hispanic. What I wanted is for these Hispanics to grow strong in this country and to get the education that is available . . . it isn't our fault that we were born in developing countries where there is sometimes poor education. I don't want them to feel guilty, but I did want them to learn English."

Mercedes's service within the Church has been as varied as it has been impactful. From nurturing the youth to serving alongside her husband for 9 years as 1st Counselors of the Washington DC North Mission, her faith has been the crucible in which her capacity to love and lead has been refined.

Through eight decades of witnessing and weathering change, her conviction remains unshaken; "Faith is what helped me go through life's challenges. Because I had faith in the Lord, I had faith in the Gospel. and I have the companionship of Holy Ghost. I have found happiness. I learned to smile. The gospel is the most wonderful thing that has happened to me. It strengthens my knowledge that Jesus is the Christ, the Savior of the world. He taught all of us how to love, be happy and he gave us the best example to follow."

||||||||||||||||||||||||||||||||

Merecedes Lorenzana resides in Maryland, US with her husband. She continues to be involved in the Hispanic community and engaging with her 4 children and many grandchildren.

Fully Anchored
in Jesus Christ

Susan H. Miller

||||||||||||||||||||||||||||||

Susan Miller has always drawn from the strength her mother and grandmothers instilled in her and has used that to face challenges in her life. She confronted considerable friction when she continued her education as a married woman and young mother in the '60s, but relied on personal revelation to confirm that she was on the right path. She earned her bachelor's degree in English at BYU and later returned as a graduate student and then as an adjunct professor. Despite unpleasant dealings with Church leaders and members of past wards, Susan learned to change her perspective and focus on Christ in order to overcome friction.

Susan's worldview was expanded by her family, which didn't fit the common mold of their Rexburg community in southeastern Idaho. Despite her father being an inactive member of the Church and her mother being a nonmember, Susan and her siblings regularly attended church and were baptized.

"As babies, our paternal grandfather blessed us," she told me. "We attended Primary starting at age three. Each of us children were baptized when we were eight. We were taught to pray, had prayer in our home over meals, read scriptures, and were expected to listen to General Conference dressed in Sunday clothes."[1]

"Key to my personal approach to much that has to do with the Church is that I learned, even as a young child, to take a step back and take the lay of the land," she said. "My maternal grandmother, for example, wasn't a member, but was one of the most spiritual, religious people I've known."

Susan recognized that while her grandmother did not share the same faith, she was an extraordinarily positive influence in her life.

"She was a teacher and better educated than others in our small farming community, so although not LDS, she was highly regarded," Susan recalled. "She was kind and loving, full of vigor and enthusiasm for life, and patient with her grandchildren. Her influence for good in my life is inestimable. My paternal grandparents, members of the Church, were much the same."

At church, Susan met people like her grandparents, who were kind and positive, but she also met some who were not. She felt that some were prejudiced against the few nonmembers and inactive members in their community, such as those

----

1. (Miller 2023)

in her nuclear family. She saw that there was both good and bad within as well as outside the Church.

"To the point: I learned that not being a member of the Church doesn't make you deficient, and that being a member of the Church doesn't make you better or more loved by Christ," Susan said. "I learned, in other words, to take things in stride. And more, I instinctively learned along the way to set my internal compass on Christ and the restored gospel."

Growing up, Susan also learned to look to the women in her life for examples of diligence and hard work. Even in eras when it was uncommon for women to work outside the home, Susan's mother and grandmothers all did so, and they taught Susan to blaze her own path. Susan's mother was an English professor at Ricks College. Her maternal grandmother was also a teacher and came from a family that valued education and prioritized it for all their children, regardless of gender.

"My mother grew up in that atmosphere, so she passed it on to us as well," Susan said. "It wasn't typical of the area where we grew up."

Susan's paternal grandmother also served as an example to her. She had lived in Los Angeles with her husband, a police officer, and their two young children. He was killed when she was only twenty-seven years old, and she moved back to the farming community in Idaho where she'd grown up.

"She went to work her entire life to support her family," Susan said. "I saw that role model."

Not only was her family influential in prioritizing education and a career for Susan, but they also showed her by their words and actions that women were not valued less than men. Susan's father, particularly, acted in partnership with his wife.

"He took the initiative in jumping in and helping with things around the house," Susan said. "He was as good a cook or better than my mom. This was in a day and age when it was not heard of."

This upbringing allowed Susan to grow up without internalized prejudice.

"I never did think women were a little bit less than men; that thought was never in my head," she said. "And this may be one of the most heretical things an LDS woman can say, but I do think that there are LDS women who—even if it's subconsciously—think that way, because they're acting that way. 'My husband has the priesthood, so he is in charge and can do everything and I have to ask permission to do anything.' You know, that was sort of the milieu I grew up in, but that isn't what I've seen in my family."

The lessons Susan learned from her family regarding education and equality would prove invaluable to her when she encountered friction later in life. When she received her patriarchal blessing, she was told that it was important for her to pursue her education. She took that advice to heart, even after she got married in 1966 and was expected to stay at home.

"I did know that I was doing something a little like swimming upstream when I stayed in college as a newly married young woman," Susan told me. "My husband and I are both from the Rexburg area and went to Ricks College. And this was very, very typical: you graduated from high school, you got married young, you stayed home, and you had children. And that was simply the pattern. And I did get married young, but I stayed in school. . . . There was never a question in my mind that I was going to stay in school."

Susan and her husband transferred to BYU. She gave birth to their first child in November, during midterms, and her professors supported her and let her make up her exams. Despite the academic support Susan felt, her community within the Church was not as positive.

"It was my church community, my ward community, where I felt that silent wall of pushback," she said. "I was really in the outhouse with our student ward in our church community. For example, I had a doctor's appointment one day and my husband couldn't come home. I asked my visiting teacher if by any chance she could watch my son for about an hour while I went to the doctor's appointment, and she just kind of brushed me off and said, 'Oh no, I can't do that. I think I have some things to do today.' And maybe she did, maybe she didn't, but that was the sort of treatment I was getting from the ward family—but not the BYU family at all."

After graduation in 1969, Susan and her family moved to California when her husband started graduate school at Stanford. The culture there was a far cry from what she had experienced in Provo.

"I thought the world had changed," she said. "At Stanford it felt like, 'Wow, you admire me for what I did—for staying in school and doing this against a lot of hard odds.'"

One thing that particularly struck me during my interview with Susan is the incredible role models she had. Because of them, it felt natural for her to continue her education and keep moving forward. When I asked how she was able to feel comfortable in her chosen path even when it bumped up against cultural norms, she said that her family's examples had taught her to follow a path that felt good for her.

"I'd like to be one of those really faithful women who said I made it a deal of great fasting and prayer, but I didn't—I just moved along a track that I had started when I was young," she said. "It felt right."

Susan also pointed out that what worked for her may not work for others, and vice versa. She told me she learned to give others the space to have a different path.

"I was able to say, 'It's not right for you. This isn't what you want to be doing. But it's right for me,'" she said.

"We were coming off the civil rights movement, deep into the Vietnam War, and there were protests around the country," she recalled. "While we were at BYU, we were vaguely aware of BYU being referred to as an island of tranquility in a sea of chaos. You didn't hear any talk about social unrest in Provo, Utah. And as far as the Vietnam War went, which was ripping the country apart, we were aware of the shootings at Kent State University, but it was literally like we were in this little bubble world."

Susan recalled that in the 1970s, women at BYU still had to wear dresses and dress shoes on campus, and her first walk around Stanford was a stark contrast.

"You go walking around hippy Stanford, it was all new and exciting," she said. "It was like, 'Oh, there's a different world out here from BYU.' But I think that's what Stanford opened up for me: just a willingness to look at different viewpoints."

Experiencing various places, people, and cultures can enrich our lives and broaden our understanding of our journey here in mortality. But that only happens if we allow ourselves to open up and challenge previous beliefs and reframe them based on new experiences. Susan did that at Stanford and expanded her ability to think critically and find the truth.

During that time, there was a clear narrative in the Church that a woman's role was to stay home with her children. However, as I've shown in previous chapters, not all LDS women felt that was what God genuinely wanted them to do. Susan managed to balance caring for her six children with her pursuit of education and teaching. She built on experiences she'd had early in her life where she had studied things out, prayed for guidance, tried to find answers, and moved forward until she received more light. Now as a grandmother of twenty-seven and great-grandmother of seven, Susan sees clearly how she has built on experiences she had early in her life.

"If there's something I don't agree with or I have a question about this, I'm going to study about it," she said. "I'm going to pray about it. And if I don't get an answer, I will put it back on the shelf, and I will take it out again later. Maybe at a later time, there's more information and I am able to get more revelation, and I will get an answer, but I might not. And that goes back on the shelf again. I think that's a healthy attitude to have."

The first time Susan ran into cognitive dissonance in the Church was regarding polygamy. She was unfamiliar with the Church's history of plural marriage, and when a friend of her husband's started making jokes about Brigham Young's many wives, she was shocked.

"They couldn't believe I didn't know," she said. "I think I had heard the word 'polygamy.' But that really shook me."

Susan steadied herself and figured there was more to the story that she needed to find out. Over the years, she did; she learned more about it and studied the issue at length.

"I think there were some abuses with polygamy," she told me. "But by and large, even though it was hard for the women, and I think harder than what some people can still acknowledge, I think it was one of those things where they did what they had to do in spite of a lot of the pain and heartache that went along with that."

The first time Susan ran into something that didn't make sense about the institution of the Church, she studied it out herself. Gradually, over years of searching, she came to a balanced place on that question. She continued to do the same with other issues. For instance, when the Church came out in opposition to the Equal Rights Amendment, Susan was upset by the doubling down on gender roles within her community.

"I learned very quickly to be quiet and to just go about living my life." she said. "By then I had completed my MA and was teaching on the adjunct faculty in the English Department at BYU. There was just a lot of trouble brewing and boiling over in the community as a whole, and I kept my own counsel."

Susan didn't put her head in the sand; she marched forward on her unique path. She recognized the friction, worked on it, studied it, and kept moving.

"I hear people talk a lot about reconciling opposites," she said. "And I am of the belief that . . . you have to be willing to hold a paradox in your head. At some point, I might see or find a reconciliation, and if I don't, I've got to be OK with that."

We have already seen that during the application of an emphasis from the Church, there can often be less than optimal implementation because of the inherent opportunity for individual local and regional ecclesiastical leaders to interpret based on their own world view. Susan had a difficult experience with this, but she was able to draw on her ability to see clearly and to keep her focus on the Savior. At the end of our conversation, Susan told me about a painful experience that would forever cement her focus on the Savior.

"I got a call from the executive secretary to set up an appointment to see the bishop," she recounted. "I thought, *Well, he's going to call me to be a Relief Society teacher again.* And so I went, walked in, and I immediately knew something was wrong, because there was no greeting. His face was so angry, and he just motioned me to a chair. And he started in on me. His message just took me aback—I was startled.

"And I just sat there and listened to him go on about my job, how unfaithful I was, what an apostate I was, how I was leading others into apostasy. And on and on he went, and the charges came fast and hard, one more outrageous than the next. He became very personal. It was too much of a vitriolic attack instead of a factual, 'Here is how I see you acting and behaving.' He even accused me of beating my children with a ball bat. And

I just sat back, and I thought, *This man can't think logically that I beat my children with a ball bat; I don't beat them at all. I don't spank them at all.* And I just sat there staring at him thinking, *What alternate universe did I just enter?'*

The bishop told Susan he was going to excommunicate her, and she could no longer remain quiet.

"I had learned through my life to be a docile Mormon girl," she said, "and I had learned to not lean in. But I do remember leaning forward ever so slightly in that moment. And I said, 'What proof do you have of any one of these charges? I don't know much about Church courts, but I have heard that you must have solid proof and even witnesses when an excommunication Church court is held.' That kind of rattled him, I don't think he expected that. He kept raving on and finally, he said, 'I just want you to know that if I want to excommunicate you, I can.' And I said, 'I want you to know that you had better have rock-solid proof before you ever bring in excommunication charges against me.' And I got up and walked out of the office.

In a daze, Susan drove her car around for two hours, trying to process what had just happened.

"I drove just to collect my thoughts, because my head was still just swirling, like, *What just happened here?* And finally, I calmed down and I came home. I didn't say anything to the kids, but I told my husband, and he just said, 'The bishop shouldn't have done that.' But here's what happened on that two-hour drive. I was befuddled at first and then I was very, very angry. Who in the world does this bishop think he is to do this? And all of a sudden, I had a thought—it was like a light bulb. I thought, *Whose church is this? Oh, yeah, of course. It's Jesus Christ's church.* And I thought, *I can't pin my testimony and my being a part of Christ's community on any bishop or any human being. This is Jesus Christ's church.* I have known that since I was a little girl, and He is the one I have to focus on. And that centered me—it stabilized me. And that is what I think all the time."

Susan knew that her bishop's inexcusable behavior was an aberration; the experience did not sour her on bishops in general.

"By and large, bishops are really good, decent man who are trying really hard to do a very, very, very difficult job," she said. "And once in a while you will have a rogue bishop—you'll have a bishop who's a pedophile, you will have a stake patriarch who has an affair with a woman in the ward. And so, what are you going to do, leave the Church? I took my stand that day. I've had things happen to me along the line. But I hope that this is the one that has me fully anchored in Jesus Christ, because that is where I have to be."

This experience with her bishop was a pivotal moment in Susan's life. She looked at her situation and drew strength from the Savior. Instead of focusing on the unfairness of the situation and wanting that to change, she broadened her worldview and used that to double down on her own sense of purpose.

I learned from Susan that when we face difficult situations that include cultural stances, or even situations growing out of power dynamics in the Church, we need to take a step back and remember why we are members, does that benefits outweigh the inherent flaws. It is up to each of us to receive our own personal revelation for our course of action, to be willing to hold a paradox in our minds, to allow and embrace changes in the way we see the world. As we do, we can grow like Susan and become fully anchored in Jesus Christ.

‖‖‖‖‖‖‖‖‖‖‖‖‖‖‖‖‖‖‖‖‖‖‖‖‖‖‖‖‖

Susan Miller resides in Provo Utah with her husband. She is an avid reader, active grandmother and mother who loves the outdoors.

Conclusion

Friction is not going away anytime soon. As frustrating as it can be, it isn't a mistake; friction exists by divine design. It allows us to exercise our agency in order to learn and to grow. The women I interviewed understand that, and they have used friction as a source of momentum throughout their lives. As I spoke with these women, I found several recurring themes in positively dealing with friction.

The first is finding connection with women of the past. Learning about our foremothers allows us to take a step back from our current cultural situation and associated biases and see things from a different perspective. As we study how others before us dealt with friction, we can apply the principles they used to our own time. This connection to women who have gone before us is nothing short of a majestic thread tying us all together across space and time.

A clear point that resonated with most of the women is learning how to receive and recognize personal revelation. It gave each of them self-confidence, security, and peace with their chosen unique paths. It also blessed each to be able to educate in her sphere of influence using her authenticity, her talents, and her voice. From Elizabeth Hammond pursuing a medical career in Utah, to Christine Durham advocating for women's rights in the face of fierce opposition during the ERA movement, to Melba Kooyman putting together her own LDS women's articles to educate those around her, these women exemplified finding confidence from their own revelation.

Each of these women in their own way found that there were inherent benefits by participating in the LDS church, which outweighed the friction that inevitably would come from being in an organization. The ability to serve, the opportunity for rubbing shoulders with people that disagree with you, and the weekly rituals that remind us of our place in something bigger than this mortal self, were benefits that these women valued.

As we saw with Susan Miller, Nora Cummings, and Kathleen Flake, sometimes man's implementation of a God-given principle isn't entirely correct, but being able to rely on personal revelation helps one identify the true principles at the heart of it all. This allowed these women to realize that we are all just trying our best despite our flaws, and that God allows and encourages our imperfect efforts. He isn't ironclad in His requirement of perfection, because if he was, he wouldn't have humans implementing his principles.

Another common thread was that none of these women let the friction in their lives be all-consuming. There's an old saying that we are viewing the world through a straw—we see so little of it. Just think: If your vision is narrowed down to only focus on one piece of friction, that is all you will see. Your vision becomes smaller, your anxiety rises, and the problem becomes all-consuming. I learned from these women to not let the one or two (or three or four) points of friction decrease my view of all the beauty and majesty of God's plan.

One of the key takeaways for me was that women who stayed in the faith felt their responsibility was to live authentically to their own internal compass. Although their paths might not have reflected what they heard at the pulpit, they did feel a responsibility to model, articulate and advocate in their sphere of influence for women (and all humans) to follow their own unique paths while partaking of the benefits of a faith community. Through education and modeling, they had a sense that progress could happen with regards to the narrative of what a woman of faith looks like. But ultimately, they didn't let the lack of progress weigh them down to a complete stop. They kept in mind that this is the Lord's Church; that means it's *His* job to fix it. We have to live true to ourselves, to be authentic and articulate within our sphere of influence, to serve Him and others as He directs us, but none of us have the ultimate responsibility to "fix" the Church.

Leaders come and go. There is an ebb and flow, and change does happen. After meeting with all these women, I have found myself wondering what I will look back on in a few years. Will everything have worked itself out? What will become the new points of friction? My key learning is that friction will be constant. There is no bow to be tied on the present of the Church or any organization; it is an ever-evolving gift from God.

Friction is our friend. It teaches us about ourselves and smooths out our rough edges in order to allow us to move and grow faster. As we learn to embrace it, it will allow us to become more like Christ.

Bibliography

African Americans and the Church of Jesus Christ of Latter-day Saints. 2023. (January 1). https://www.blackpast.org/special-features/african-americans-and-church-jesus-christ-latter-day-saints/#1589229840341-e7154bc4-871d.

Black, Susan Easton, interview by Robin Ritch. 2023. (March 29).

Bradley, Martha Sonttag. 2005. *Pedastals & Podiums: Utah Women, Religious Authority & Equal Rights.* Salt Lake City Utah: Signature Books.

Bushman, Claudia, interview by Robin RItch. 2023. (March 16).

Bushman, Claudia, interview by Robin Ritch. 2023. (March 16).

Bushman, Claudia Lauper. 2003. "My Short Happy Life with Exponent II." *Dialogue: A Journal of Mormon Thought,* Fall: 183.

Cummings, Nora, interview by Robin Ritch. 2024. (January 19).

Derr, Jill Mulvay, interview by Robin Ritch. 2023. (April 12).

Durham, Christine M, interview by Robin Ritch. 2023. (March 4).

Dushku, Judy, interview by Robin Ritch. 2023. (March 18).

First Presidency of the Church of Jesus Christ of Latter-Day Saints. 1976. "First Presidency Statement on the ERA." *First Presidency letter*. Salt Lake City, Utah: *Ensign Magazine*, October 22.

Flake, Kathleen, interview by Robin Ritch. 2023. (March 27).

Hafen, Bruce and Marie. 2018. *Faith is Not Blind*. Deseret Book.

Hamilton, Carey Holwell. 2016. *Wyoming Black Fourteen 1969*. September 1. https://www.blackpast.org/african-american-history/wyoming-black-fourteen-1969/.

Hammond, Elizabeth, interview by Robin Ritch. 2023. (April 11).

Kooyman, Melba, interview by Robin Ritch. 2023. *Connections to Women* (April 5).

Lorenzana, Mercedes, interview by Robin Ritch. 2024. (January 29).

Miller, Susan, interview by Robin Ritch. 2023. (April 12).

Peterson, Grethe Ballif. 2022. *Growing Into Myself*. Salt Lake City, Utah: Grethe Ballif Peterson.

Phillips, Marilyn, interview by Robin Ritch. 2023. (March 29).

Poelman, Anne Osborn, interview by Robin Ritch. 2023. (February 27).

Rees, Robert. 2011. *Why I Stay: The Challenges Discipleship for Contemporary Mormons*. Salt Lake City: Signature Books.

Relief Society Organization Timeline Relief Society Organization Research Guide. 2023. https://history.churchofjesuschrist.org/training/library/relief-society-organization-research-guide/relief-society-organization-timeline.

Saints, The Church of Jesus Christ of Latter-Day. n.d. *IMPORTANT EVENTS IN THE History of Relief Society*. https://www.churchofjesuschrist.org/study/manual/daughters-in-my-kingdom-the-history-and-work-of-relief-society/important-events-in-the-history-of-relief-society.

Silver, Cherry Bushman. 2021. "The Early Development of Latter-day Saint Women's History An Interview with Jill Mulvay Derr." *BYU Studies Quarterly*, Volume 60, Issue 4: 93–96.

The liberation of being myself. 2021. (December 10). http://ldswomenproject.com/interview/the-liberation-of-being-myself/.

Ulrich, Laurel Thatcher. 1981. "The Pink Dialogue and Beyond." *Dialogue: A Journal of Mormon Thought*, Winter: 28.

Vivanco, Anabella, interview by Robin Ritch. 2024. (January 2).

Author's Note

I had wanted to interview a diversity of women representing different ethnicities, but in the 1970s the pool of LDS women who were participating in the Church and choosing careers was limited. Since ERA played out only in the United States, I was limited to the U.S. population, and non-white people made up an infinitesimally small percentage of members of the Church. Finding women who were still alive, who had been members in the Church during this timeframe, was extremely challenging. The lack of racial diversity in my interviews represents the makeup of the Church during that time.

Acknowledgments

||||||||||||||||||||||||||||||||||

This book would not have been possible without the advice, help, and encouragement of so many others. First of all, without Christine Durham none of this would have happened. One word describes her: formidable. Had she not been such an articulate, transparent, intelligent, and kind person, I never would have embarked on this journey to find out what these amazing women went through and how they kept their faith. Thanks to my editor, Elayne Wells Harmer, who brought life to what I wrote in a manner I could not. I'm indebted to my friends who gave me access to places of peace to draft this book: Heidi and Randy Jenson, Ann Maas, Amy Veater, and my parents. Thanks also to Ann Maas for her unwavering support of this project, brainstorming, and reading it to make sure I made sense. Thanks to Jonathan Johnson and Elizabeth Ingersoll who helped find some of the overlooked voices found in this book. Thanks to my friends who continued to ask and prod me into finishing this book: Mindi Rich, Kady Day Lieber, Barbara Brown, Sally

Steed, Emily Bell McCormick, Kristin Andrus, Susie Wheeler, Candace & Greg Osborn, Joanna Ho, Carrie Sheffield, and Jennifer Thomas. Thank you, my family of origin and the imprint that has been forever, left on me by their example. Just as these women benefited from community, I too have been affected by the communities that have allowed me to think, discuss, and learn with them. I am forever grateful for my women's discussion group and for my time in China, Del Mar, Palo Alto, Oregon, and Seattle, where in each place I found a community of women with whom I could learn and grow. I also want to thank my nieces and nephews—because of them, I could picture my book's intended readers.

Robin Ritch is a transformative leader and strategic advisor known for driving growth across startups, high-growth ventures, and global corporations including Microsoft, Intel, and Cisco. She most recently served as President and Publisher of Deseret News Publishing Company, overseeing both editorial and business functions at Deseret News, Church News, and Utah Business. In this role, she repositioned a 172-year-old regional outlet into a nationally recognized voice, significantly expanding its reach through digital transformation and strategic innovation.

Robin's career reflects a consistent ability to identify opportunity, mobilize resources, and deliver measurable impact. She has launched and scaled new products, modernized operations, and convened diverse communities around meaningful conversations. Beyond her professional achievements, she is committed to community impact through service on nonprofit boards including The Policy Project, WikiCharities, Wasatch Innovation Network, and Mission Edge. For decades, Robin has also been deeply engaged in studying women in relationship to God—a passion that informs her writing and leadership.

Robin holds a BS in Finance from Brigham Young University and an MBA from the University of Washington.